135 1858年 The Harris Treaty
136 1855-1800 日本从学习蒸汽机技
39-41 福泽谕吉的著作
142 1864年他创办了 Yokohama Spe
243 Keio Gijuku 创立于1868, 主
144 Keio 最注重物理, 其次是经济; 它的商科也是 way 到...
147 福泽谕吉: 人需要修身; 自由是人在满足自己时不伤及别人
151 福泽谕吉认为孝应基于自然的情感 (作者此处未展开)
161 孟子对抱怨的看法
165 福泽谕吉认为高度文明无法在一个只求利的社会中保存
60 福泽谕吉于1875年将 nationality 翻译为国体
67 福泽谕吉于1875年左右认为国体的根本并非历史, 而是独立, 历史是维系国体最
重要的因素
73 福泽谕吉认为皇宫与之附近必须极尽豪华, 平常人的生活见不到
76 福泽谕吉认为责任感比自力更重要
82 福泽谕吉认为人回归了至善的本性就能达到 ultimate values
76 福泽谕吉认为男女应该平权; 1885年 他提出女性应受教育, 地位要提高
7 福泽谕吉认为家庭应该独立, 所以结婚后夫妻要抛弃原来姓氏
93-95 西方人对儒家以及中国文化的批评
97 江户时代的教学机构
00 福泽谕吉认为教育与政府应分开
05 作者认为孔子收学费. 福泽谕吉认为让人自由与独立的提"实学"
06 福泽谕吉认为中等阶级由开智的武士领导, 由向学的工、商组成
2 儒学让中国避免了帝国主义
8 作者认为在儒学中经济发展是衡量政府的指标?
9 "舜禹之有天下也而不与焉" 被作者认为是儒家范围理想.
13 1884年时, 日本还没有 a uniform system of measurement
14 福泽谕吉与其学生深受 Francis Wayland 的道德、经济思想.
15 福泽谕吉认为有钱就可以控制舆论
16 福泽谕吉认为无商人是在大格局上贪婪
19 儒家认为人生而平等
34 福泽谕吉认为当时的日本要保护自己的商品; 鄙视中国人?
36 儒家的"等级"基于道德

P142 福泽谕吉认为日本人太依赖"仁心"，不够独立

P144 福泽谕吉认为要让西方人尊重，日本需与中国和朝鲜不同

P145 福泽谕吉认为军事强大才最重要

P146 福泽谕吉认为当时世界的"道"就是杀或者被杀。

P147 另一方面，福泽谕吉也认为要遵守国际法

P148 福泽谕吉认为日本应该派兵去朝鲜保护它的独立

P150 福泽谕吉认为日本妇女应出国工作来为日本谋利

P151 福泽谕吉认为中国人向满洲尽忠。

P153 福泽谕吉认为儒家阻碍中国的发展，要让中国走向近州得超过满清

P157 孔子与福泽谕吉的比较，作者犯了个错误（！）

P168 作者对儒学的总结☆

P173 福泽谕吉的思想并不统一

P175 西村茂树认为儒家思想很不错，但误解它的人因为尤其它的名字而无法了解
   实质

# Fukuzawa Yukichi

The Pioneer of East Asia's
Westernization with Ancient
Confucianism

# Wei-Bin Zhang

PublishAmerica
Baltimore

First printing

PublishAmerica has allowed this work to remain exactly as the author intended, verbatim, without editorial input.

Hardcover 978-1-4489-3143-9
Softcover 978-1-4489-5007-2
PUBLISHED BY PUBLISHAMERICA, LLLP
www.publishamerica.com
Baltimore

Printed in the United States of America

# Table of Contents

# 3

# 4

# *Preface*

Fukuzawa Yukichi (1835-1901) is a famous Japanese scholar, an educator, a newspaper publisher, and a writer of immensely popular books and essays on the West, the founder of Keio University, and the father of public speaking in Japan. He was born into a low rank samurai family. In his funeral, fifteen hundred mourners, marching four abreast, accompanied his body from his home to its final resting place. One of the most important contemporary management thinkers, Peter Drucker, describes the importance of Fukuzawa for Japan's modernization as follows: "the key to understanding this [the Meiji Restoration] was the THREE men...Fukuzawa Yukichi, Shibusawa Eichi and Iwasaki Yataro. I do not think it an exaggeration to say that between themselves these three men created modern Japan, and with it much of the modern world altogether."[1] Liang Qichao (1873-1929), a most important Chinese thinker in modern times, once remarked on Fukuzawa, Voltaire and Tolstoy as follows; "If these men had not lived, it is doubtful whether their countries could have advanced."[2] Fukuzawa was also appreciated as follows: "So wide-spread is the influence exercised by this remarkable man that no account of Japan, however brief, would be complete without reference to his life and opinions."[3]

Fukuzawa has made a deep and lasting impression upon the modern Japanese. His photo and name in Japanese are globally circulating as they are printed on the 10.000 Japanese Yen note. "Here lies," the epitaph on a monument to him reads, "a man of self-reliance and self-respect with a world-wide vision." Nevertheless, irrespective his importance for understanding modern Japan, there are only a few comprehensive studies of Fukuzawa from the perspectives of East Asian civilization in the English literature. Except his *Autobiography* translated into English by his grandson Kiyooka Eiichi, only a few English books are available on his thought in a comprehensive sense.[4] In *Recent Philosophical Thought 1862-1996*, Piovesana argues that Fukuzawa's "interesting personality truly deserves a comprehensive study in a Western language."[5] This book examines Fukuzawa's thought and ideas from a new perspective. We demonstrate that Fukuzawa is the first East Asian thinker who systematically modernized manifestations of the essence of the ancient Confucianism—through accepting Western practices for an industrializing economy and discarding traditional East Asian manifestations of the neo Confucianism in the three agricultural economies, China, Korea and Japan.

East Asia has increasingly attracted attention from various fields of intellectual pursuits. Many scholars tried to explain Japan's success in modern times from various perspectives. Scholars are still arguing about why Japan is the first non-Western country to adapt the Western values, institutions and technology. "Thoughtful scholars drew up a list of attributes that might provide an answer; this list included Japan's supposed ethnic and cultural homogeneity, its geographical position close (but not too close) to the Asian mainland, wet-rice agriculture, a neo-Confucian work ethic, a national history of selective institutional borrowing from the outside, and so on."[6] I have argued that in all these interpretations the possible impact of the essence of the ancient Confucianism upon Japan's modernization has been neglected.[7] Japan received its higher culture from China for most of the past two millennia.[8] The most important thought system in Chinese civilization is Confucianism. If the essence of Confucianism is suitable for modern societies, one may find Confucianism a positive factor for explaining why Japan had been rapidly transformed from a traditional Confucian civilization into modern one. I will show this point by studying Fukuzawa and relating his thought and ideas to the ancient Confucianism.

Over more than 100 years, it has been commonly believed that Fukuzawa was anti-Confucian. This book challenges this popular opinion by demonstrating that his vision and thought about civilization and society had no conflict with the ancient Confucianism. We will show that Fukuzawa had timely modernized manifestations of the ancient Confucianism. He actually claimed himself a follower of the ancient (classics) Confucianism in the following way: "But should my forebears' words and deed be truly in accord with Confucianism, then I, too, am a believer in Confucianism with no vestiges of doubts."[9] My deviant travail examines what he meant by "a believer in Confucianism", basing on my recent studies and interpretation of the ancient Confucianism in a systematic manner.

This book is not merely a study of Fukuzawa *per se*. It is a consequence of my efforts to apply modern (Western) knowledge to interpret East Asia's thought systems and East Asia's Westernization/ modernization. It is a part of a broad study about Confucianism and its implications for modernization of the Confucian regions (covering Mainland China, Taiwan, Hong Kong, Macao, Vietnam, Japan, South Korea, North Korea, and Singapore). In *Japan versus China in the Industrial Race* (Zhang, 1998), I examine issues related to why Japan could have so rapidly become industrialized and why China had been so slow in its take-offs within a broad perspective. It is shown that Japan followed the Confucian principles when faced with economic, political, and military challenges from the West and China had been against the Confucian principles. In *Confucianism and Modernization* (Zhang, 1999), the Confucian principles are summarized in contemporary terms. It is shown that the important elements, except masses voting processes, of democracy can be identified in Confucianism. Instead of voting, China used the examination system

11

to select right men to govern. In *Adam Smith and Confucius* (Zhang, 2000), the ethical, social, and economic principles advocated by Adam Smith and Confucius are compared. It is demonstrated that they are similar in principles but different in their 'sentimental emphases'. In *Singapore's Modernization* (Zhang, 2002), the role of Singapore government in economic development and democratization is examined in perspectives of Confucianism. In particular, the influence of socioeconomic geography on the Singaporean Chinese's individual and group behavior and mind is addressed. It examines why Singapore is unique among the Confucian regions where the government explicitly emphasized the Confucian values. In *Taiwan's Moderniza-tion* (Zhang, 2003b), I interpret the rapid democratization of the Chinese community in terms of socioeconomic geography, Confucian tradition, and the American influence. The books on Taiwan and Singapore show how different environmental conditions have influenced the modern politics, the mentality, and the economic development of Chinese immigrants. In *The American Civilization Portrayed in the Ancient Confucianism* (Zhang, 2003a), I show that the essence of (the ancient) Confucianism does not include elements for clashes of Confucian and American civilizations as, in an almost arbitrary manner, claimed in *the Clash of Civilizations and the Remaking of World Order* by Samuel Huntington. In *Hong Kong – The Pearl Made of the British Mastery and the Chinese* (Zhang, 2006), I examine why Hong Kong has been rapidly industrialized under the British governing. The book shows that the Chinese who had been under the Manchu governing with the neo-Confucianism had become a disciplined, obedient and docile "servant" of a rational ruler even before the British began to govern Chinese in the island. The combination of the Manchu-neo-Confucian servile spirit and the British rational governing explains how the "pearl" was created. In *New China's Long March from Servility to Freedom* (Zhang, 2007), the history of China after World War II has been explored from perspectives of the ancient Confucianism. This book tries to provide a unique and challenging interpretation of Fukuzawa's thought from the perspective of the ancient Confucianism.

# 1

## The Pioneer of Modernizing Manifestations of the Ancient Confucianism

It is generally held that Fukuzawa Yukichi (1835-1901) was the most influential expert on the West in Japan in his lifetime. No other Japanese scholar so clearly recognized and explained the need for Japan to change its traditional values and practical morality. According to Blacker, Fukuzawa was "undoubtedly the most comprehensive exponent of the doctrines of Enlightenment. No other scholar pointed out so caustically the incompatibilities of the old ways of thinking with the needs of the new age."[1]

Fukuzawa was prominent educator, writer, and propagator of Western knowledge during the Meiji period (1868-1912), founder of Keio Gijuku (now Keio University), and founder of the newspaper *Jiji Shimpo*. He also modernized the art of public speaking in Japan. His collected works, written over a period of 30 years, fill 22 large volumes and cover a variety of subjects ranging from philosophy to women's rights. Even when his countrymen had little idea about the West, he had begun to explain almost every important thing in Western civilization. He had persistently demonstrated that if Japan were not to become westernized and become strong enough to be a match for the Western nations, it would suffer humiliations under the Western powers like India and China had. He had tirelessly taught the whole nation that it was not sufficient to have large guns, large ships, and a new government. Japan had to change in its spirit and way of thinking. He consistently asked Japanese people to rethink some of fundamental assumptions upon which the Japanese society had been constructed.

He is also known for his negative attitude towards the so-called Chinese learning in Japan. In an era when the Chinese learning was the main school of thought, he advocated for avoiding the Chinese learning and making efforts to produce a new generation of leaders versed in Western science and the spirit of independence. He is generally looked on positively as having played an important role in the modernization of late 19th-century Japan. At the time of his death the Japan Weekly Mail valued his contributions to the nation's Westernization as follows: "The Tokyo newspapers…declare that nearly every Japanese subject who has attained any eminence during the Meiji era owes something, directly or indirectly, to his instruction or influence. He is described as the great motive force of Japan's modern civilization; the man who did more than all his contemporaries to promote the spread of a spirit of true liberalism."[2]

When he was young, Japan's education was based on the neo-Confucian teachings. The neo-Confucianism had been applied to justify the monopolistic power of the emperor in China. He was against the fastidious formalism and rigidity of the doctrine. He argued that the Confucian education was an obstacle to modernizing Japan. He found that there were two serious problems in the Confucian teachings: "the lack of studies in "number and reason" in material culture, and the lack of the idea of independence in the spiritual culture. He further argued that education in sciences and technology and the spirit of independence are essential for Japan to survive. If Japan wanted to assert itself among the strong nations of the world, Japan had to develop science and technology and cultivate the spirit of independence. Rather than recognizing that Japan had failed to correctly learn from the Chinese learning, He blamed Chinese culture as follows: "Chinese philosophy as the root of education was responsible for our obvious shortcomings."[1] When he referred to Confucian teaching, he often meant the neo-Confucianism. It is obvious that traditional Chinese learning does not contain modern science and technology. Nevertheless, Confucianism is not against "number and reason". In fact, the positive attitude toward "number and reason" is reflected in *I Ching*, which is a classic of Confucianism. Although the traditional manifestations of the neo-Confucianism in China and Japan do not encourage the spirit of independence, as we will show, the ancient Confucianism does not lack the spirit of freedom.[3]

As he had been educated in the ancient Confucianism before he began to learn Western civilization, it is important to examine possible influences of the ancient Confucianism on his values and knowledge structure. This study demonstrates that his rapid adoption of Westernization is not without cultural continuity of Confucian civilization. Indeed, it is difficult to conclude with certainty whether or not his main thought and ideas were directly influenced by the ancient Confucianism. Nevertheless, we disclose that the principles he advocated to Japan are congenial to the principles of the ancient Confucianism, which he was familiar with. In *Questions on Moral Education* of 1882, he explained his attitude towards Confucianism, saying that it is not because the Confucian principles are invalid for modern society, but what Confucianism asks people to do would not satisfy the mainstream of the public opinions. According to Fukuzawa, what matters in society is not the essence of principles but popular opinion. His success was largely due to—except his understanding of different thought schools—his talent in following and influencing the popular opinion. As he believed that the public opinion is the key factor of socioeconomic development, manifestations of the ancient Confucian principles should be modernized in order to play a positive role in progress of civilization: "my wish is to let...Confucius's teachings be absorbed into the principles of independence, because this is the time when moral teaching will undoubtedly be changing according to popular opinion."[4] He held that the ancient principles should be adapted to the current mainstreams of society and popular opinion. Moreover, if these principles are not suitable for some areas, they should be discarded. This viewpoint is important for us to appreciate his thought as it implies that on one hand, Japan should keep the essence of the classical principles (ancient Confucianism) so that there is a cultural continuation in essence and don't need to blindly change the essence of Confucian civilization, and on the other hand, Japan should adapt or design new rules, laws or habits for creating a modern society. This viewpoint is reflected in the historical fact that in contrast to cultural destruction in modern China,[5] Japan's modern development is characterized of cultural continuation and Westernization.

Although he admired the ancient Confucianism, he did not hold that Japan had been correctly applying the principles in his time. In his 1886 *On the Association of Men and Women*, he pointed out that the principles of the ancient Sage had been first correctly applied in society in forming the guiding percept of the people and national customs. He also observed: "The Sage's original intention must have been to maintain a pure and faithful moral attitude in the people. But today, has the Sage's purpose been fulfilled? I fear that the result has been the reverse."[6] He argued that the traditional manifestations of these principles were not suitable for the time. In the same article just cited, he held that the Sage's words are not wrong as they were effective in his time, but "The fault lies with the scholars of subsequent generations who did not adapt the teachings to their own times but simply handed them down word for word." He argued that the future generations did not correctly follow the rules, adding more restrictions on the original rules. Finally, the elaborate rules had become ineffective on guarding moral behavior of the society.

Fukuzawa often used key Confucian words in expressing his Westernized thought in spite his severe attack on Confucianism. Nevertheless, we should distinguish his criticism of Confucianism as a feudalistic doctrine and Confucian learning as an academic study. In fact, many scholars of Meiji enlightenment, including Fukuzawa, held that the Confucian concepts and sayings had facilitated the absorption of Western ideas and played an important role in helping Japanese people to quickly understand and appreciate Western civilization. "For Fukuzawa, it is one thing to evaluate Confucius and other Confucians as scholars, and another to criticize the social and ideological function of their ideas .... His way of criticizing Confucianism, which attaches importance to its functional role rather than its academic substance, is also utilized in his accepting Western civilization."[7]

By the ancient Confucianism, in this book, we mean the Confucian doctrines developed by Confucius, Mencius (371-289 BC), and Hsün Tzu (298-238 BC). In order to order to show what we mean by that Fukuzawa modernized manifestations of the ancient Confucianism, it is necessary to introduce the principles of the ancient Confucianism and examine his basic thought. We say that Fukuzawa modernized manifestations of the ancient Confucianism if the essence of his ideas and thought is the same as the essence of the ancient Confucianism. It is in this sense that this book considers him as the pioneer of modernizing manifestations of the ancient Confucianism. In analyzing the Confucian views on key aspects of Fukuzawa's thought and ideas, we quote generously and exclusively from these three ancient thinkers. The exclusiveness is not only because these three are the most original and important thinkers in Confucianism, but also because their ideas were constructed in an era when multiple cultures communicated with, learnt from, and emulated each other. They had life experiences in different cultures and served heterogeneous governments. They did not perceive a world controlled by the emperor or a single government.

Fukuzawa passed away more than hundred years ago. Japan is still honoring and remembering him in different forms such as conferences and seminars on his thought and publications about his life and thought, not to mention his photo on the 10,000 Yen bill. "History has to be rewritten in every generation," Hill assets, "because although the past does not change the present does; each generation asks new questions of the past, and finds new areas of sympathy as it re-lives different aspects of the experiences of its predecessors."[8] After having lived in Japan for many years and having been concerned with Westernization of Chinese people in different parts of the world, I feel "driven" to re-examine his thought and ideas not only because what he advocated had led Japan to speed up Westernization but also because his thought and ideas do explain the "mental growth processes" of Westernization of Chinese people as well. This book demonstrates him to be the pioneer of modernizing manifestations of the ancient Confucianism in East Asian civilization.[9]

# 2

# Life, Learning and Social Activities

*He gives increase to others without taking from what is his own – he obtains his wish on a grand scale.*
*I Ching: Sun*

Civilization is a process of man's rise from a near animal state to a human society featuring exercise of reasoning, creation and adoption of civilized values and technology, and cultivation of arts. History shows that the movement of a society towards a civilized state depends on two factors: the intellectual power of outstanding men to conceive sound socio-economic ideas and theories and the ability of majority to properly apply these ideologies. If the hosts of common men have a taste for bad ideas, nothing can prevent social disasters. In modern times, China's prolonged processes of take-offs were closely related to its choice of Marxism instead of Confucianism or Capitalism as state ideology; while Japan's swift adaptation to modern civilization was much due to its taste for rational Western ideas. To do this, this study examines the formation of ideas and thought of Japan's most influential intellectual, Fukuzawa, during Japan's early modernization.

Fukuzawa lived between 1835 and 1901, a period which comprised greater and more extraordinary changes than any other period in the history of Japan. He recognized that if Japan was to avoid humiliating experiences that India and China had suffered under the Western powers, Japan must have modern guns, ships, Western law, and Western social and economic organization. Having seen the piecemeal devouring of Qing dynasty China by the Western powers, he taught Japanese people that Japan should not suffer the same fate. He was one of the first Japanese to travel to the US and to Europe. He was enthusiastic and skillful at conveying ideas to others. He did provide a model for the men of his era in the next step towards adapting Western culture to Japan. He was the most comprehensive exponent of the doctrines of Enlightenment before World War II in East Asia. He was unique in East Asia to point out so drastically the incompatibilities of the old East Asian ways of thinking with the needs of the new age. None in East Asia explained so clearly and so properly the need for new values and practical morality in ordinary, everyday life. In order to know the formation of his ideas and thought, we first study his family and social environment.

## Brought Up by His Mother in Poverty

Fukuzawa was born into the family of an impoverished low-ranking *samurai* of the Nakatsu domain (now part of Oita Prefecture) in Kyushu. The social order of his father, Fukuzawa Hyakusuke, was barely high enough to have a formal audience with the lord. Hyakusuke was the overseer of the treasury. He spent much of his time at his lord's storage office and headquarters in Osaka. All his children – Fukuzawa, his three sisters, and one elder brother – were born in Osaka. Fukuzawa, the youngest child, was born on January 10, 1835, when his father was 43 years old and his mother 31 years old. Fukuzawa was only two years old when his father died in June 1837. Soon, his mother took the five children back to Nakatsu.

Like Confucius and Adam Smith,[1] his father died when he was only two years old. Also like Confucius and Adam Smith, he was brought up by his mother through hardship. His father was a Confucian scholar. He was very good at writing classical Chinese as well as poetry. Although he was a clan official, he was a scholar, a literary person, and a poet. Fukuzawa admired his father. "Because I was unable to serve my father while he was in this world, I am ever careful not to tarnish his name and reputation after his death....I learned all about my late father's words and deed in great detail from my mother while she was living."[2] He thought that his father died with discontent. He felt that the feudal system was his father's mortal enemy. He was very sorry for his father because he died young without realizing any desire in his life because of the feudal system. In *A Bequest of Old Coins to Children* published in 1896, he described his father to his own children: "He studied in the school of Ito Jinsai and Togai, father and son, who specified in scholarly analyses of the Chinese classics....His interest was widespread, his mind capable in a large variety of subjects, never inclined to a single direction." Although his father would like to spend a quiet scholarly life, he had to engage in worldly affairs, bargaining with merchants and negotiating loans for his lord. He disliked what he was doing. He tried to provide his children proper education. His mother told him that his father hoped that he would exceed his class status and become an important person. When he was a baby, his father often said to his mother that when he grew up, his father would send him to a monastery and make him to become a priest. This was what his father could expect best for him because at that time the law of inheritance ruled that sons of high officials followed their fathers in office, sons of foot-soldiers always became foot-soldiers, and those of the families in between had the same lot over years without change. The strict laws of the Nakatsu clan required that in almost every context of daily life, the lower *samurai* should abase themselves before their superiors in feudal rank. The men in Fukuzawa's status were much poorer, less educated, and more tediously occupied than the upper *samurai*. The former also had to address their superiors with honorific words; while the latter replied the former in habitually abusive language. Marriage between the low and the upper was strictly forbidden and virtually unknown. In his childhood, people accepted all the distinctions of feudal rank as though they were part of the natural order – no one could change it. As his father had no opportunity to rise in society, he could only wish that his youngest son might find a good life through the priesthood. Fukuzawa's hatred of the traditional class system was seeded when he was a boy.

He spent childhood as a member of the lower *samurai* class in a small, caste-bound village. In his childhood, he did not mix with other children in Nakatsu. The family had little contact with the neighborhood. The children of his family spoke Osaka dialects. Also, their mother dressed them up in Osaka way, which appeared quite queer to the eyes of local people. The children played themselves; they never got along with any of children in the neighborhood. Nevertheless, the home life was happy. This perhaps partially explains why he tended to be unconcerned with ways of society The children did not quarrel among themselves and they seldom made their mother annoyed. The mother made great efforts to teach her five children manners. His mother did not seem to have any religion. She was independent and showed a great sympathy towards poor people. In his early days, Fukuzawa did not have true friends outside his family. The distinctions between high and low were made not only on official occasions, but also in the private intercourse, and not only among adults, but also among children. Children from low *samurai* families had to use a respectable manner of address in speaking to the children of high *samurai* family, and the latter would speak to the former with arrogance. In school, he was best at study and physically strong. But once out of the schoolroom, he was inferior. In later years, he would advocate that nothing but learning and ability should be used to determine one's social status. His sociality had never gone to the extent of opening himself completely to the confidence of others. He did not share with others in the inner thoughts of his thoughts. "I was not taking my acquaintances too serious,"[3] Fukuzawa recalled.

Even when he was a boy, he did not care much about feudal propriety. He did not have any reverence for the things generally accounted holy. Once, he tried to test its efficacy, he trampled on the sacred paper charms and put them to vile uses in the lavatory. Since his childhood, he loved to read books. Besides this love, he had also been accustomed to working with his hands, such as handling planes and chisels and making and mending things. He did not seem to be interested in any art. Fukuzawa said about himself: "I possess little of what people call 'good taste.' I care nothing for the kind of clothes I wear or the kind of house I live in."[4] He said that he even did not understand why fashions in dress varied over time. Once his brother asked him what he intended to do in the future when he was a young man, he replied that he would like to be the richest man in Japan and spend all the money he wanted to. "I decided", Fukuzawa recalled his earlier life, "not to compose poems and purposely to remain unskilled in calligraphy. This peculiar whim of mine was a great mistake. Indeed, my father and my brother were both cultured men....When it comes to antiques, curios, and other branches of the fine arts, I am hopelessly out of it."[5] He said that he could not have the pleasures in finer education. It seems that he considered "finer education" only useful for pleasure rather than as an important part of cultivation.

As the second son in the family, Fukuzawa had no right to succeed as household and inherit the duties in Japan's patriarchal feudal society. All the main duties of the family belonged to his elder brother. He inherited the household duties only after his brother died. Before his brother's premature death, he was free to leave home and go to Nagasaki in 1854, and then Osaka to learn Dutch. In September 1856, his brother died at Nakatsu when he was studying in Osaka. He returned home to help his family. He became the head of the family. He had to perform certain duties to his lord according to the position of his family in the feudal system. But his mind was never in Nakatsu, even though he obediently carried out every act of filial and feudal obligations. He decided to go to Osaka again. He tried to convince her mother that he should leave the hometown for Osaka because he had studied Dutch in Nagasaki and Osaka and had confidence in being successful with his Dutch learning. "If I stay here in Nakatsu, I shall never be able to distinguish myself."[6] By this time, all his sisters were married and his mother was living only with a little granddaughter of three years, left by his brother. Irrespective of her own difficulties, his mother allowed him to go to Osaka to pursue Dutch learning.

Before he left for Osaka, he had to pay all the debts of 40 *ryo* left by his brother. He and his mother decided to sell everything of his household, including his father's large collection of books. There were over fifteen hundred volumes in the collection, among them some rare ones. His name, Yukichi, was taken from the second syllable of a rare book of the Ming dynasty. Having sold almost everything of the household, he finally paid the debts. Among the very few things unsold, he kept the classic of the Chinese classics, *I Ching* (*the Book of Change*), the treasury of his father. The book was annotated by Ito Togai, the scholar his father most respected. According to Fukuzawa (1899: 46), his father had written in the catalogue of his books: "These thirteen volumes of Ethics [*I Ching*] with Togai Sensei's notes are a rare treasure. My descendants shall preserve them generation after generation in the Fukuzawa family."[7] As become evident late on, for those who are familiar with the "*I-Ching* way" of thinking, his ideas would appear much less inconsistent and self-contradictory than they are claimed to be.

In the late 1861, he married Toki Okin, whose father, Toki Tarohachi, was a Nakatsu upper *samurai* of the first rank. He was a permanent resident in Edo assisting the ministerial office. According to the Tokugawa tradition, a marriage between the low and upper *samurai* families was almost impossible in the Nakatsu domain. As Tamaki pointed, this was partly due to Fukuzawa's diplomacy and skill in handling human relations. For instance, he could deliberately impress and even please Toki Tarohachi by sending him a letter from San Francisco.[8]

Soon after he returned from San Francisco in the autumn of 1860, the *bakufu* asked Fukuzawa to serve provisionally as an officer at the translation departments of foreign commissioners. He liked the job because he could use the *bakufu* library, which held many English books. The job also offered him other opportunities to pursue English learning. From the early 1861, he began to translate diplomatic letters. In the later 1864, he officially joined the *bakufu* translation department.[9] But he did not take any government post in his life since the Meiji Restoration, even when he was invited to. By the time of his death he was a national figure, with former pupils in all walks of life, and revered as one of the founders of the new Japan. He did not like to be involved in government job mainly because he disliked the arrogance of officials. He considered that to be an official was to join a foolish game as when an official might bully below him, he must at the same time receive the bullying of those above them. He did not want to become an official also because he could observe and laugh as a private person, but he had to play with those ridiculous pretensions if in office. Another reason kept him from the government was that he held that the average official's moral standard was low. These officials were promoting civilization on the one hand, but they were practicing the debased customs of the old on the other hand. He felt that these officials were below his standard and practice. He had some affairs with officials occasionally but he would not work under the same roof with them.

## First Learning the Ancient Confucianism

As his mother had to do all the housework, education of the five children was largely neglected. When Fukuzawa was about fourteen or fifteen years old, he found that many of boys of his age were studying at school. He began to join the class of oral reading of *Mencius*, while other boys of his age had already advanced to the stage of discussing the Chinese classics. Because of his talent, he soon found himself in the class of discussion. Under Master Shiraishi, he made rapid progress. After four or five years, he had learnt much the Chinese classics.

It is generally believed that Confucianism had been introduced to Japan in the 5th century. Before the twentieth century, Confucianism was important during the 6th to 9th centuries and from the Edo period (1600-1868). During the Tokugawa period, there were broadly three categories of learning: (1) Confucianism, which had a distinguished pedigree and possessed great prestige; (2) Japanese learning (*kokugaku*), which arose in the mid-Tokugawa period; and (3) Dutch learning (*rangaku*) which sprang up as an adjunct to medicine and gradually spread to other areas, such as language, astronomy, geography, physics, chemistry, and military science. Two of the three fields were alien in origin. Tokugawa society created what we now know as "traditionally Japanese". Irrespective of its seclusion policy, Japan was not totally secluded. Japan remained in contact with China and Holland, the homelands of the two alien studies, throughout the Tokugawa period. During the seclusion period, Japan had collected information about China and the West. Chinese books, including Chinese translations of Western works, were imported every year from China. Japanese students of Dutch learning also learned many of the modern scientific advances in contemporary Europe and America. Before he first traveled to the West, he had accumulated much knowledge about Chinese learning as well as Western knowledge.

Confucius, the founder of Confucianism, did not write original works. It is traditionally believed that he edited the following texts: *I Ching*, basically a manual of divination; *Shu Jing* (Book of Documents), a collection of historical works; *Shi Jing* (Book of Songs), an anthology of early song texts; *Li* (Ritual), a ritual text no longer extant; and *Chun Qiu* (Spring and Autumn Annals); and a brief history of Confucius's own state of Lu. In addition to these texts, there were *Lun Yu* (Analects), a collection of sayings by Confucius and his disciples; Xiao Jing (Classic of Filial Piety); and a number of commentaries and ritual compendia including the influential *Li Ji* (Record of Ritual). These texts constituted the Confucian canon. During the Song dynasty (960-1279), Confucianism underwent a revival and development known as Neo-Confucianism, and it was in this form (mainly, the Cheng-Zhu school) that it was destined to become most widely studied in Japan from the 13th or 14th century. In Japanese it is usually referred to as *Shushigaku* (the Zhu Xi school). This system gave rise to a school of divination and a body of literature that dealt with directional taboos. It was contrary to the rational spirit of Confucius's teaching, yet it exercised great influence on the lives of the Chinese as well as the Japanese. In Japan, Confucianism received official recognition under the third Tokugawa shogun, Iemitsu (r 1623-51), and its position was further improved under the fifth shogun, Tsunayoshi (r 1680-1709). The eighth shogun, Yoshimune (r 1716-45), encouraged diffusion of Confucian teachings among the non-*samurai* urban population. Shogunate patronage of Neo-Confucianism underwent an important development during the period of the Kansei Reforms (1787-93). Ideological uniformity was imposed in 1790 by prohibiting all but Cheng-Zhu teachings. Nevertheless, it should be noted that traditional Japan did not make Confucian learning the basic qualification for bureaucratic office. Confucian education did not become an important path to highest office in Japan, as it did in traditional China. The university functioned instead to train middle—and lower-ranking officials whose birth normally denied high rank and office. Confucian meritocracy made almost no progress against the predominantly hereditary occupation system in Japan. The *samurai* were not dissuaded from their martial values by Confucian civilian ideals.

Toward the end of the seventeenth century, a number of private scholars challenged the Cheng-Zhu teachings. These men rejected much of the neo-Confucian system of metaphysics and self-cultivation and advocated a return to what they held to be pristine Confucianism. They are often grouped together under the name of *kogakuha* (School of Ancient Learning). The earliest major figures in this tradition include, for instance, Itō Jinsai (1627-1705), who taught a practical ethics based on benevolence, loyalty, and faithfulness. He held that the path of the sages should be understood by direct readings in such Confucian classics as the *Analects* or the *Mencius*, and he discouraged reliance upon later interpretations. His studies are generally referred to by the name *kogigaku* because the aim was the clarification of the original meanings of the classics. *Kogigaku* is considered part of the *kogaku* (Ancient Learning) school. His rejection of neo-Confucianism was consolidated and given a political thrust by Ogyu Sorai (1666-1728), who urged rigorous philological study of the classics to enable an adaptation of the institutions created by the ancient sage-kings of China to the ordering of contemporary society. He attacked the entire neo-Confucian tradition and insisted upon returning to the Chinese originals of the Six Classics—the Five Classics plus the *Zhou li* (Rituals of Zhou). He held that the language of the neo-Confucianists was different from that of the classics. For him, the Way was not innate, but was "constructed" by the sages.

We will show that if one admired the ancient Confucianism, one should be against the neo-Confucianism because of its lacking of the sprit of individualism. Fukuzawa had been educated in the Confucian classics and strongly influenced by Western civilization. This is important for us to understand how he could have criticized the neo-Confucian practices in Japan, Korea and China. Fukuzawa's knowledge of Chinese learning is said to be important for him to grasp differences between Western and Eastern civilizations as well as to explain the formation of plain and attractive writing style with high sprit.[10] His teacher at Nakatsu did not believe in neo-Confucianism and emphasized Confucian classics.[11] The influence of Chinese classics is also reflected in his influential book, *Gakumon no Susume* (An Encouragement of Learning).

Fukuzawa had a good knowledge about Chinese language. His first book was a translation of Chinese-English dictionary into the Japanese. When he traveled to the US, he purchased two dictionaries in San Francisco bookshops. One was the *Webster's Dictionary*. The English was too difficult for him as he was only a beginner in English. The other book was a Chinese-English dictionary edited by Zhi Qing. He worked hard for a few months in translating the dictionary. He published the dictionary in 1860 as *Enlarged Chinese-English Dictionary*. "This was the prolific Fukuzawa's first publication….It is almost certain that Fukuzawa did the translation to enhance his capacities in English."[12]

We will show that his adoption of Westernization was not without cultural continuity of Confucian civilization. Even though he might not carefully read ancient Confucian classics after he began to pursue Dutch learning, in his 1878 letter in reply to Nakamura Rituen, he revealed his view on the Confucian classics in the following way: "If you regard my father as a person who endeavored to follow and study Confucianism and was assiduous in literature activities, then I am the son of that very person, and I earnestly admired and believe in his words and deed."[13]

## Changing from Chinese Learning to Dutch Learning

In the 16th and early 17th centuries, English, Dutch, Portuguese, and Spanish merchants and missionaries brought to Japan objects of Western material culture, such as clocks and firearms, as well as Western technical skills, such as navigation and surgery. But due to the Tokugawa shogunate's (1603-1867) policy of National Seclusion, by 1639 the Dutch were the only Westerners permitted to enter Japan—a limitation that continued for about two centuries. During the first century of seclusion, it was principally the official interpreters of the Dutch language at Nagasaki who became versed in Western culture. Although the Japanese authorities severely restricted personal contacts with the Dutch, the Japanese thirst for knowledge of the West persisted—sometimes even among the authorities themselves. Near the end of the 18th century, some Japanese scholars started to warn of foreign threats, first from Russia and later from Britain, France, and the United States. Shogunate leaders also recognized the need to acquire much more systematic knowledge of the outside world, and in 1811 they appointed officials to translate foreign books. Military science became the most important field of Western Learning in the 19th century due to the impending foreign threats.

By the early 1800s, Japan actively engaged in Dutch studies. In 1815, Sugita Gempaku published *Rangaku kotohajime* (the beginnings of Dutch studies). Sugita described how Dutch studies had been spread in Japan in earlier days: "At present, Dutch studies are in great fashion throughout Japan. Those who have decided to pursue them do so avidly, although the ignorant among the populace praise and admire these studies in greatly exaggerated terms."[14]

Tokugawa Japan had gained knowledge of Western science. Fukuzawa expressed his indebtedness to the Dutch studies tradition for his later achievements. During his 1860 visit to America, Fukuzawa was not much surprised at modern developments of technology such as the telegraph and metalworking.[15] By this time, Japan already began to avail itself of Western science and technology. He knew that the development of Western science and technology was not a product of blind chance but due to efforts of scholars started a century ago before his time.[16] The eighteenth-century pioneers in Dutch studies were aware of negative influences of Chinese learning. Sugita doubted about Chinese learning and observed: "Was it not because our minds had already been trained through Chinese learning that Dutch studies were able to develop this rapidly?."[17] When Fukuzawa set about the study of Dutch very early in life, Dutch studies had become popular in Japan. From an early age, he disliked what he regarded as the narrow stiffness of the feudal domain. In February 1854 when he was 20 years old, he left Nakatsu and set out to Nagasaki. By this time, no one in Nakatsu could understand the "strange letters" written sideways, even though there were students studying the Dutch language in large cities. The coming of Commodore Perry had warned the Japanese about the coming problems of national defense and the modern gunnery even in small towns. His brother told him that anyone who wanted to gunnery and the Western science seriously had to study the Dutch language and asked him whether he liked to study it. He described his own decision: "I will study Dutch or any other language. If other people can learn it, I think I can too."[18] As he admitted, his confidence came from that he did not feel any difficult in learning Chinese. Mainly because he wanted to get away from Nakatsu, he soon went to Nagasaki to study the Dutch language. But he studied only irregularly and under many teachers. He stayed in Nagasaki only one year.

After one year since he left Nakatsu, he went to Osaka to meet with his brother. He soon found a good teacher of Dutch learning in Osaka. In 1855, he joined the Tekijuku, the celebrated school in Osaka for Dutch studies. The school was run by the physician and teacher of European medicine and Dutch learning, Ogata Koan (1810-1863). Ogata was born in Bitchu Province (now part of Okayama Prefecture). He first studied medicine in Osaka and in 1831 moved to Edo, where he studied Dutch, basic science, and medicine. In 1836 Ogata went to Nagasaki for study with a Dutch doctor, and in 1838 he opened a school of medicine and Dutch Learning in Osaka, the Tekijuku, which was immediately successful. Fukuzawa, Omura Masujiro (1824-69), Sano Tsunetami (1822-1902), Otori Keisuke (1833-1911) and others who played important roles in Japanese society after the Meiji Restoration of 1868 studied at the Tekijuku. Ogata's Fushi Keiken Ikun, a translation of a German text on internal medicine, was widely circulated in handwritten copies. He also led an effort against smallpox. In 1862 he was appointed physician to the shogun and head of the Tokugawa shogunate's institute of Western medicine.

At the Tekijuku, Fukuzawa studied the Dutch language with enthusiasm. He also showed great interest in any branch of Western science—chemistry, physics, or anatomy. He worked very hard that he did not even have a good night's rest for a whole year. Osaka at that time was a city of merchant devoted to internal commerce. Hardly anyone wanted to be informed on Dutch gunnery or Western arts. There was little demand for work and knowledge that Fukuzawa and other students mastered. Nevertheless, they studied hard foreign texts for no clear purpose. "Yet not one of them [Fukuzawa and his fellow pupils] knew or cared whether Dutch would prove useful to them in later life. They flung themselves into the task because it was difficult, and for its own sake."[19] Fukuzawa found great pleasure in pursuing the

Dutch learning. He was proud of the fact that he was a possessor of the keys to knowledge of Western civilization. He described: "If our work was hard, we were proud of it, knowing that no one knew what we endured. 'In hardship we found pleasure, and the hardship was pleasure.'" [20]

He spent three years and seven months at Ogata Koan's school. [21] His reading of Dutch books and scientific training at the Ogata School had given him enough of a background in natural science to facilitate his understanding of the explanations of the latest inventions made in America. But he could not interpret social, political, and economic phenomena observed in America with his Dutch learning. In fact, there were only 10 Dutch books in the Tekijuku library, all of which were on physics and medicine. Except Ogata, there was no qualified teacher. All classes, except the highest grade, were taught by senior students. The school was a place where students did nothing but copy, read and translate the ten books. The largest school of Dutch studies at that time did not have any staff except Ogata and the rest was all students. But, in the school, Fukuzawa found himself in a new world. It was the first time in his life that he felt "liberated". Within the school premises, family lineage, wealth, and social status were not important. What counted were students' ability and scholarship.

## Giving up Dutch Learning and Pursuing English Learning

A man moves upwards; a dog does not take a dislike of poverty of its master.
Chinese proverb

By the 1850s, American interest in Japan coincided with the increased whaling activity of American merchant ships in the Pacific. Yet whenever assistance was needed along the coast of Japan, American ships and sailors did not receive 'proper treatment'. Internationally, after the arrival of Commodore Perry and his black ships in 1853 and the forced opening of the country, many Japanese saw their way of life threatened by the foreigners and the gap that lied between Japan and the West. Many saw a need for political change and for adopting Western technology for military and industrial purposes to be able to compete with foreign countries. The feeling of having to keep up with the West was widely spread. Domestically, the shogunate and powerful *daimyo* vied with one another to buy or build Western-style ships and guns as Japan approached the civil war that led to the Meiji Restoration of 1868. In the 1860s, Japanese began to abandon Dutch studies and Dutch language and started to study English.[22] Soon English became the primary Western language for Japanese intellectuals. Fukuzawa was to become a pioneer in the study of English in Japan.

In 1858 when he was 25 years old, Fukuzawa was asked to leave Osaka for Tokyo. An official in service at the headquarter of his clan at Tokyo was interested in Dutch culture. Under his influence, a school of the Dutch language was opened in the estate of the clan in Tokyo. Since he had finished his studies in Osaka, he was asked to teach in the school. This was the beginning of his career in education. The small school he started later grew into Keio Gijuku and finally to Keio University. One day in 1859, he visited the new foreign trading community in Yokohama, one of the Japanese ports that were opened to foreigners under commercial treaties Japan signed earlier with five nations. He was surprised that what he spoke no foreigner could understand and what foreigners spoke or wrote he had no idea. He found that the foreign merchants did not speak Dutch. He felt depressed when thinking of how many times he had spent on Dutch learning.[23] He was very disappointed as he had made great efforts in Dutch learning and had a great confidence in being as one of the best in the Dutch language in the country. He recalled: "It was a bitter disappoint, but I knew it was no time to be downhearted."[24] The main foreign language at Yokohama was English. He soon realized that English language and studies of Britain would become a must in the future and he changed his interest to studying English. Soon after he returned from Yokohama, he started to study English. Since then,

English became an important tool for him to learn from Western civilization.

Fukuzawa first studied Chinese and then Dutch. Now, he decided to learn English. As there were few Japanese teachers of English available at the time,[25] it was almost impossible for him to find a proper English teacher. He decided to study English by himself. He bought an English-Dutch dictionary. He translated English writings into Dutch every night. It did not take him long to achieve a high level in reading English, because of his efforts and similarities between Dutch and English. In 1860 he joined the first Japanese mission to America, and two years later, he joined the first Japanese mission to Europe. These tours also helped him understand English words, which were not fully explained in dictionaries. Immediately after his first travel to America, he wrote: "The American tour fortunately enabled me to contact directly the people there and obliged me to commit myself to English learning. After coming home, I worked hard to read English as much as possible and abandoned teaching Dutch to my students."[26]

Although his ability to read and comprehend English books was excellent, he was not very good at speaking English.[27] He studied English, emphasizing on reading at the expense of pronunciation or communication skills. In fact, his style would soon become the norm among Japanese English learners, as it was believed to be a quick way to learn the language. His English was proper for his own purpose because all he needed at that time was to be able to comprehend English books. His goal was to absorb Western concepts, translate related writings and help those who had no knowledge of English comprehend circumstances in the West.

**The Travels to the West**

Before the Meiji Restoration in 1868, Fukuzawa made three visits to the West. He soon shared his experiences of Western civilization with a wide range of people including revolutionaries and merchants by writing three volumes on conditions in the West (1866, 1868 and 1871). He introduced the political, economic and cultural systems, and histories of various western countries, basing on his overseas experiences. In his two subsequent important works, *An Encouragement of Learning* (1871-1876) and *An Outline of a Theory of Civilization* (1875), he explained the characteristics of scientific technologies and cultures of the West.

In 1859, the Japanese government decided to send a "ship of war" (which was a small sailing craft equipped with an auxiliary steam engine of one hundred horsepower) to the United States. The vessel, named *Kanrin Maru*, was purchased from the Dutch a few years before. Since 1855, offices had been studying navigation and the science of steamships under the Dutch residents of Nagasaki. Now the council of the Shogun had decided that Japanese officials and crew take a ship across the Pacific to San Francisco at the occasion of Japan's first envoy's departure to Washington. The *Kanrin Maru* was to escort the envoy who, was sailing on an American warship, *Powhatan*. In 1860 Fukuzawa joined the first Japanese mission to America (Man'en Kembei Shisetsu). The 81-man shogunate mission sent to Washington, DC was to ratify the United States-Japan Treaty of Amity and Commerce of 1858 (Harris Treaty). The Harris Treaty was the first commercial treaty between Japan and the United States, signed on 29 July 1858. The American consul general, Townsend Harris, arrived in Shimoda in August 1856 to secure provisions for free trade, which the Kanagawa Treaty, signed in 1854, lacked. In December 1857, Harris had an audience with the shogun in Edo. Thereafter, he negotiated with shogunal representatives and by 25 February 1858 had secured a draft treaty. A formal treaty was finally signed without imperial sanction. The treaty stipulated the exchange of diplomatic agents and consuls; the opening of various Japanese ports; the right of American citizens to reside in those ports, trade without interference, and enjoy extraterritorial privileges; the opening of Edo and Osaka for trade; and a moderate, fixed scale of import and export duties. Similar treaties were concluded within a few weeks with the Netherlands, Russia,

Great Britain, and France. The unequal terms of these treaties and the Harris Treaty plagued the shogunate for 10 years and then the new Meiji government until 1899, when a new treaty with the United States went into effect.

The group of shogunate officials and domain representatives left Japan in January 1860 aboard *Powhatan*. The *Kanrin Maru* accompanied the *Powhatan* to San Francisco. The young Fukuzawa was on board as one of the mission's interpreters. He felt very proud of the accomplishment for his own country. (Japan saw a steamship for the first time in 1853 and started to study navigation from the Dutch in 1855. By 1860 Japan was already able to sail a ship across the Pacific.) It took only a few years for the Japanese to master the new technology with helps of foreign experts. He specially noticed that no other people of the Orient could achieve this. He believed that "there is no other nation which has the ability or the courage to navigate a steamship across the Pacific after a period of five years of experience in navigation and engineering. Not only in the Orient would this feat stand as an act of unprecedented skill and daring."[28]

When the ship came into the port of San Francisco, the Japanese were greeted by many important personages. Along the shores thousands of people were lined up to see the newcomers. "Our welcome on shore", Fukuzawa described, "was certainly worthy of a friendly people. They did everything for us, and they could not have done more. The feeling on their part must have been like that a teacher receiving his old pupil several years after graduation, for it was their Commodore Perry who had effected the opening of our country seven years before, and now here we were on our first visit to America."[29] "Before leaving Japan, I, the independent soul…had feared nothing. But on arriving in America, I was turned suddenly into a shy, self-conscious, blushing 'bride'."[30] Before he sailed back to Japan, he bought a copy of Webster's dictionary. This was the very first importation of Webster's into Japan. He mentioned that once he secured this dictionary, he felt no disappointment on leaving the new world and returning Japan.

The Japanese were greatly impressed by the American ballot system. In Washington the mission met with President James Buchanan and exchanged documents on 17 May. The mission left the United States in August 1860. Two years later, when he was 29 years old, he joined the first Japanese mission to Europe, visiting France, England, Holland, Russia, and Portugal, and learning all he could of Western civilization. He spent 44 days in England, 42 days in France, 20 days in Germany, 35 days in Holland, 20 days in Portugal, and finally 60 days in Russia. On 9 May 1862, he sent a letter from London to a senior official of the Nakatsu domain (who was residing in Edo), explaining what he wanted to do in Europe: "I have resolved to do research by looking closely into the conditions and customs of European countries. I have…made queries about the institutions of their countries, military systems, taxation and so on. …There is no way but to buy books.… The entire sum I have been given in Edo as allowance will be spent in purchases of books."[31]

A year later since he started his journey to Europe, he returned to Japan with an immense wealth of observations, knowledge and books. During his visit in Europe, he tried to learn some of commonplace details of the European cultures. He did not study scientific or technical subjects while on the journey, because he thought that he could study them as well from books after being back to Japan. As he described in his *Autobiography*, he emphasized learning daily life of the people because the Europeans would not write these common matters in books and it was important for Japanese people to know them. He described his observations about democracy in Europe. He noted the co-existence of different political parties and special was amused at that the Liberal and the Conservative were always fighting each other in the government. In *Autobiography*, he described what he felt after he received a friendly treatment in London. He knew surely that among Western peoples one could find people who were truly impartial and warm-hearted. These observations about positive aspect of Western civilization had made him more confirmed about the importance of free intercourse with the rest of the world. In *Seiyo jijo* (Conditions in the West), he summarized his observations of Western governments: they followed liberty, promoted religious toleration, encouraged trade and development of arts, roads, schools, and education, valued peace and security, and maintained benevolent institutions for the poor, the sick, and the needy.

After returning from Europe, he traveled abroad only 4 years later. He returned to the United States, visiting Washington D.C., Philadelphia and New York. He was sent as an envoy to negotiate on behalf of the Japanese government, but his personal aim was to acquire textbooks to take back to Japan. He was able to upgrade his school curriculum with the books he bought back from America. On 27 July 1867, he returned back to Japan. Fukuzawa was blamed for demanding commission for his selection of books in English for the *bakufu* and for bringing back his own books on board the return ship without paying any shipping charges. Fukuzawa was thus put to house arrest. He returned to normal work by the end of November 1867.[32]

During his travels in the West, he carefully observed the Western societies and made efforts to bring information as much as possible back to Japan. "Fukuzawa's *Account of My Voyage to the West* and *Notes on My Voyage to the West*", observed Hirakawa, "are full of memos scribbled in a hodgepodge of Japanese, Dutch, English, and French. A glace at these works shows Fukuzawa to be a virtual walking antenna, eager to absorb any and all information in these foreign lands."[33] He tried to observe different social aspects of reality in the Western civilization and explain them as an integrated whole to illustrate why the society was functioning well as a whole.[34] He had an open mind not only to the Western civilization. In *Words Left in Nakatsu* in 1870, he taught that not only books form different countries of the West and Japan must be read with great care, but also Chinese books and books from India. "The argument on the merits and demerits of different schools is something that should come after one has accumulated knowledge....In taking up a subject, one should first consider the advantage it will bring to our country rather than the merits and demerits of the school itself."[35]

## Scholar, Educator and Writer

After returning from the travels to the West, he began to introduce Western civilization to Japan. The information he collected on his journeys to the West formed the basis of his celebrated work *Seiyo Jijo*. Before its publication, the Japanese public had no way of learning about Western people or institutions and culture because the Western knowledge had been confined to medicine and related sciences. The book was a turning point for Japanese people to know about the West. The book was based on the knowledge he acquired on three trips abroad (1860-67). It was published in 10 volumes in 1867, 1868 and 1870. Volume 1 (1867) discusses numerous Western institutions: schools, newspapers, libraries, government bonds, orphanages, museums, steamships, telegraphs-in short, those aspects of modern Western life that Fukuzawa hoped Japan would emulate. Volume 2 (1868) contains translations of excerpts on governments and economics from a popular British series, *Chambers' Educational Course*. Volume 3 (1870) presents general material by British jurist Sir William Blackstone (1723-80) on human rights and by American educator Francis Wayland (1796-1865) on taxes and then supplies data on Russia and France. In these works, he tried to explain Western political systems, particularly the concepts of liberty and rights. He provided an introduction to everyday Western customs and institutions accessible to the common reader. The book was immediately successful and the sales of volume 1 reached 150,000. If one takes account of pirated editions, some 259,000 copies were sold.[36] As the size of the public reading of the time, this was a tremendous success.

This success was due to the demand for as well as the character of his work. At that time, Japanese people heard a lot about the West. The Opium War might have shocked the Japanese society much more strongly than the Chinese society under the Manchurian ruling at that time. The threat from the West was recognized real. People were also interested in everyday social institutions—such as hospitals, museums, schools, universities, railways, companies, taxation, newspapers, working conditions, social environment, social welfare, lunatic asylums – and customs, climates, and spirits of peoples in the West. He wrote the book in an unusual style at that time. It was simple and lucid and easily comprehensible by any Japanese of any degree of literacy. He made great efforts to enable his works to be read by as a wide public as possible. He had sometimes made his housemaid read his manuscripts through and would alter any word or phrase, which she found difficult to understand. The book enabled Fukuzawa to become financially independent and also provided the funds for establishing his own school. Since then, he was highly reputed as an authority on things Western. The book had a powerful influence on the Japanese public of the time. Fukuoka Takachika, a drafter of the Charter Oath and of the *Seitaisho*, the Meiji government's proto constitution, later wrote that in formulating ideas for a new political structure, he and his colleagues had relied almost exclusively on *Seiyo jijo*.

During 1872 to 1876, he published a series, collectively called *Gakumon no Susume* as an elementary-school text to modernize Japan on the Western model.[37] The work consists of 17 essays, lucidly written, appealing to a wide range of readers, including youngsters, and proposing equality and individual independence, and national independence. The title, An Encouragement of Learning, implies his assertion that one's social position is to be established by learning and endeavor, rather than by lineage. The first pamphlet began with his famous assertion that "heaven never created a man above another man nor a man below another man." He argued that wealth and honor would result only from individual diligence and study. The first volume was a bestseller of its day, with sales amounting to an astonishing one copy for every 160 people. But *Gakumon no Susume* was banned as a textbook in the early 1880s as part of a government reaction to the Freedom and People's Rights Movement and to Western influence in general, and publication ceased after 1890.[38]

In 1875, he published *Bummeiron No Gairyaku* (*An Outline of a Theory of Civilization*). The book details his theory of civilization. It was written for intellectuals in the former *samurai*-class, who had adhered to the doctrine of neo-Confucianism. It freely compares Western cultures with Japanese culture, and discusses the requisites for an independent nation in an international arena. It is still favored by many readers as one of the modern Japanese classics. According to Fukuzawa, civilization is relative to time and circumstance, as well as comparison. For example, China was relatively civilized in comparison to some of the African colonies and Australia, and European nations were the most civilized of all, at the time. This is a work of political philosophy, advocating emulation of Western spirit as a means to modernization. It is his most sustained philosophical contribution to the encouragement of Westernization. It overshadowed his best sellers *Gakumon No Susume* and *Seiyo Jijo*.

He widely explored the use of the Japanese word *enzetsu* (speech) to encourage communications. The art of debate and speech-making were alien to Japanese society at the time. He held that without effective *enzetsu*, the ultimate goal of independence would be impossible. He is commonly regarded as the father of public speaking in Japan. Oxford concludes from a comprehensive study of his speeches: "Fukazawa was an extremely capable orator." His most important contribution to the reformation effort was achieved in the form of a newspaper called *Jiji Shimpo* (Current Events).[39] He started the newspaper in Tokyo in 1882. His editorial policy was politically nonpartisan; he stressed news stories and feature articles on economics. *Jiji Shimpo* received wide circulation, encouraging the people to enlighten themselves and to adopt a moderate political attitude towards the change that was being engineered within the social and political structures of Japan. As the chief writer, he energetically conveyed his opinions on multifarious topics such as the economy, politics, society and culture. *Jiji shimpo* became a vehicle for his prolific writings. Long articles such as *Discourse on Japanese Women* (1885), *Discourse on Industry* (1893),

*Hundred Talks* (1897), and *Autobiography* (1899) were all printed in the newspaper, and then later published as books. He published not only serious articles but also satire in his own newspaper. He addressed almost all contemporary issues related to politics, domestic and international issues, political economy, education and educational policy, the moral code, women's rights. These publications fill nearly half of the twenty-two volumes of his lifetime works.[40]

During his lifetime, Japan had been swiftly transformed from an isolated feudal state to a full-fledged member of the modern world. He played a leading role during this dramatic dynamics as the educator of the new Japan and the interpreter of the ideas behind the dazzling material evidence of Western civilization to his countrymen. He used simple expressions to propagate Western civilization among ordinary people. He tried to digest the essence of Western books and translated them into Japanese in such a way that the meaning was readily evident. He used a new concept of *jitsugaku*, or practical knowledge to explain his approach to knowledge and practice. He also propounded new views of history, ethics, politics, and international relations. He proposed a new scheme of family relationships, championing particularly the cause of women. No other contemporary writer was as versatile and persuasive as him.[41] His books sold in millions of copies. This financial independence enabled him to live the life of a commoner without having to accept a position in the government. It also provided him with the means to establish a newspaper through which he could voice his opinions on current questions.

## The Founder of Keio University and Entrepreneur

Fukuzawa is known as scholar, writer, and educator. He was also one of the most successful businessmen in Meiji Japan. Irrespective of his wide involvements in business world, he has been largely neglected as entrepreneur and businessman in the studies of his life.[42] "He masterminded the establishment of the Yokohama Specie Bank in 1880, designed to attract gold and silver specie. Without the establishment of the Specie Bank, the Bank of Japan (1882) could not have been successfully founded."[43] He was also a business adviser to the Mitsubishi and to Mitsui, the old Tokugawa merchant house, enabling them both to grow into two rival but powerful groups of big firms, Zaibatsu, in the twentieth century. After the Meiji Restoration, he turned down the invitation to be an officer of the new government and played an active part outside of government. He also earned money by translating English into Japanese.

He was a school teacher for ten years in a clan school subject to the dictum of his clan. By 1868, because of the social unrest during the Restoration, the clan lost its interest in the education. By this time, he had established his vision and sense of mission to spread Western civilization to Japan. He established his own school Keio Gijuku at Shiba Shinsenza in 1868. In the 1868 inauguration speech of the school, he stated: "We have opened the doors of the school wide to the public to allow all men, regardless of their status as *samurai* or commoner, to come and participate in our program."[44] Different from the clan school where he had served as master had no systematical codes or rules, his new school had a set of regulations.

A wide range of Western textbooks were used at his school for instruction in economics, Western history, geography, natural sciences and ethics. It had soon grown into one of the leading schools of Western learning in Japan. It was not long before he brought in professors from overseas, who provided students with an entirely new educational experience. He established Keio Gijuku as an educational institution to provide an alternative to the conventional private academies, to promote higher education emphasizing science and independence, and to foster young intellectual talent. Many of these graduates became outstanding managers. By 1870 the enrollment exceeded three hundred students and in the following year, the school was relocated at Mita. Graduates of the Keio Gijuku were active in all phases of society and many of them became teachers in the new schools established throughout the country following the Meiji Restoration. The school played an important role as a teacher training center. At the time of the *Education Order of 1872*, which marked the beginning of modern education in Japan, private schools were strictly supervised and even suppressed. He was still running the school under the name *semmon gakko* (professional school).

Keio Gijuku continued to expand throughout the Meiji period (1868-1912), adding schools of finance, law, and literature in 1890, and offering the first private college-level curriculum in Japan. Around him in Keio, he drew ambitious young Japanese in growing numbers, men who were to become leaders of the new Japan in its work of political, economic, and social reconstruction. At the initial stage of the Meiji period, the new regime had not time to concern itself with education. At this time, Keio Gijugu was the only school in Japan, where any real teaching was being done. "The final purpose of all my work", he described the purpose of operating Keio Gijuku in his *Autobiography*, "was to create in Japan a civilized nation, as well equipped in both the arts of war and peace as those of the Western world." By 1898 it became the first private institution in the country with a comprehensive educational program from elementary school through college.

Among the scientific studies he promoted in his Keio school, physics stood foremost. He believed that physics was the basis of all scientific inquiry. Next to physics came economics. Keio University became a symbol for economic research in Japan even during his lifetime. He also strongly supported medical researches. Today the medical department of the Keio University, with its Rockefeller-sponsored hospital, stand near Meiji shrine in Tokyo as one of the foremost medical schools in Japan. "During Fukuzawa's life, the teaching of economics, business, commerce and finance in Keio was unrivalled by any other educational institutions including the Imperial University. The burgeoning success of Japan's economy in the last quarter of the nineteenth century was due in part to Fukuzawa's entrepreneurship."[45] The Keio University now has faculties of literature, economics, law, commerce, medicine, science and engineering, policy management, and environmental information. There are also several specialized institutes and laboratories. The university offers correspondence curricula in humanities, economics, and law and has affiliated elementary, junior high, and high schools.

In 1869, Hayashi Yuteki, one of Fukuzawa's followers, started up a trading company, Maruya. Fukuzawa invested in Hayashi's company, and encouraged his friends and other followers to join Maruya to experience the business practices of trading, especially in imports and exports. He regarded the trading company as "a business college" and a place for on-the-job-training. The company developed and grew into the famous Maruzen and Co. of today. Since its establishment in 1869, Maruzen has brought to Japan technology and culture from all corners of the earth in the form of books. As early as 1883, Maruzen began publication of Hyakka Zensho, a 12-volume series that summarized European knowledge. The series was published from 1883 to 1885. Maruzen published a translation of Chamber's Information for the people on a subscription basis, a highly unusual publishing method at the time. Today, Maruzen is firmly established as Japan's leading bookseller. Hayashi Yuteki established Maruya Shosha in Yokohama on the recommendation of Fukuzawa. Maruya Shosha was the first joint stock corporation in Japan. The following year, Hayashi opened a store in Nihombashi, Tokyo that remains Maruzen's flagship store to this day. Fukuzawa was involved in the development of the company not only by giving intellectual advice, by also making investment. Since then, his earnings from publication business had become the main financial basis of all his activities such as establishing Keio Gijuku. In connection with Maruya, Fukuzawa suggested inaugurating a number of businesses, including banking and life insurance. The banking business failed. He also lost substantial amount of his considerable investment, which was earned from his writing. His followers set up the Meiji Insurance business separately from Maruzen.[46]

In *Autobiography*, Fukuzawa described how once he succeeded in publishing business. When he began to get his writings published, he had to rely the publishers on all the business from printing to selling. He was not satisfied with some of publishers for their dishonesties. When he saw people were reading his books which he received a fixed amount of royalty, he felt pity that all the things that he could have done was only to write and deliver manuscripts and he could not get the proper amount of the money from book selling because the publishers did not pay him well. As his books had become so successful, he felt that he had lost a great deal because of his dependence upon publishers. He wanted to do publishing business himself. He had no experience in the business and had no idea about how to start it. But he knew that the first thing was to secure workmen who had knowledge and skill about how to produce books. To get experienced workmen, he first accumulated one thousand *ryo* and spent this money on buying one hundred and some bales of paper. This was a huge order since even the largest publishers would not purchase paper more than two hundred *ryo*'s worth one time at that time. Then he asked a publisher to have several dozen of his workmen. Together with some men from his clan as foremen, he put them to work in his residence. When these workmen saw how much paper was stored in his residence, they thought that Fukuzawa would employ them for the rest of their lifetime. They began to trust him and he also paid them well from the very first day of their work. As mutual trust was soon established, the workmen showed him and his clan about the tricks of trade. Since then, Fukuzawa wrote and produced his books and publishers would only sell the finished books. "This was indeed something of a revolution", he related in *Autobiography*, "in the publishing trade in our country. This is the only instance where I tried my hand in the field of actual business."[47]

# 3

## Civilization Built on Equality, Independence and Learning

My wish is to let Chou Kung's and Confucius's teachings be absorbed into the principles of independence, because this is the time when moral teaching will undoubtedly be changing according to popular opinion.

Fukuzawa[1]

For East Asian civilizations, modernization has been mainly a process of Westernization – not only in the outer realm of material culture and political forms but also in the inner realm of thought, spirit, and values. For instance, in political economy, it is not Confucianism but the thought by Adam Smith and Karl Marx that have been used as the dominant value systems. Mainland China has chosen all possible ways to destroy anything Chinese. The history of Mainland China in the last century is also a history of Westernization in Chinese soil. The so-called economic reform is a combination of the thought of Karl Marx and Adam Smith.[2] Japan is the first non-Western country that has successfully undergone Westernization. After opening their land under pressure in the 1850s, the Japanese have persistently and consistently followed the Western ways. (Japan has remained many things of its traditional culture; but these features have been considered as an integrated part of modernization rather than being against it.) Japan has now become the world second largest economy, irrespective of its lack of any natural resources, except water and limited land. Japan is politically democratic and holds the most advanced technologies in many fields. Democracy, individual freedom, egalitarianism, pacifism, and the rule of law to uphold basic human rights are the dominant values of contemporary Japan. Yet none of those ideals is derived from Japanese tradition. They all originated in the modern West. To understand how Japan has succeeded, as the first non-Western country, in Westernization, we need to understand the cultural mentality and thought that have built the modern political, legal, economic, social, and cultural systems. Fukuzawa is the most important Japanese thinker for us to understand the process of Japan's Westernization.

## "Heaven Does Not Create One Man Above or Below Another Man"

Do not regard seniority but advance the worthy and able; dismiss the incompetent and incapable without delay;... develop the common people without waiting to compel them by laws... Yet, although a man be the descendant of a king, duke, prefect, or office, if he does not observe the rules of proper conduct and justice, he must be relegated to the common ranks.
Hsün Tzu (298-238 B.C.)

According to *The Great Learning*, a Confucian classic, "Things have their root and their completion. Affairs have their end and their beginning. To know what is first and what is last will lead near to the truth." In order to explain Fukuzawa's thought as a whole, we need to study his basic ideas about individual and society. As mentioned before, when Fukuzawa was young Japanese society assumed that man was not born equally. In the Tokugawa Confucianism, it was preached that all would be fine if each of the four classes would be content with status and share of wealth as allotted by Heaven. Different from Confucian China, Tokugawa Japan fixed the boundary of social class, even though social mobility was possible within each class. Fukuzawa shocked the traditional Japanese society by claiming that all men are born equal. He began *Gakumon no Susume* with his most famous words: "'Heaven never created a man above another or a man below another,' it is said."[3] He held that all the people are born equal and all the people should work with dignity. The saying of "Heaven never created a man above another or a man below another" was a shock to the traditional Japanese society, where people's social positions were assumed to be determined by birth. This new idea is the fundamental for Japan to be transformed into a modern society.

When he claimed that men are equal, Fukuzawa did not advocate "equalitarianism". In *Words Left Behind Nakatsu* in 1870, he related: "One must cultivate moral virtues by following heaven's rule, acquire knowledge and understanding worthy of a human being, associate with people and experience things, work for one's own independence and succeed in earning a living for one's family."[4] He was also against socialist ideas.

He argued: "Here it is something that neither Chinese nor the Japanese have noted in the past: the principle of freedom and independence which exists as an inborn constitution."[5] He further explained that the term, freedom, does not imply willfulness or selfishness, but it means to act according to one's own mind without obstructing the freedom of others. Rather than the strict hierarchical social system, he argued that father and son, lord and vassal, man and woman, friends, each and all should be careful not to impose on the other. People should extend their desires freely, without enslaving any other's desires. He held that with the inborn goodness of man prevailing, no one would stray to evil ways. He strongly believed in the independence because he was strongly influenced by what he observed in his travel to America. For him, America was progressive because people were concerned with who one was rather than into whose family one was born. He criticized the traditional notion of *meibun*. This basic Confucian doctrine implied that each man possessed a *mei*, a "name" which not only defined his position in the social hierarchy, but also at the same time summed up in itself the moral qualities required by that position. All such names, in short—lord, vassal, father, son, husband, wife—were normative, not merely descriptive, defining what persons in these positions ought ideally to be, not merely what they actually were. He held that in order to establish an enlightened relationship between people and government, he argued that people should first learn "to cast off the toils of *meibun* in their own homes."[6] He believed that it was due to the doctrine of *meibun* that Japan failed to develop the spirit of independence and was faced with more problems in comparison with the rest of the world. According to him, the relationships within the family constructed with the doctrine of *meibun* had to be reformed for national development and security. The relationship between parent and children based on *meibun* demonstrated a preponderance of power, where the higher members in the hierarchy exerted an unlimited and unconditional power over the lower members. Children had certain duties to their parents simply because the parents gave them life and took care of them when they were babies. According to the Tokugawa Confucian canon of filial piety, children had to show unconditional respect towards their parents—regardless of how they were treated by their parents.

He criticized filial piety in the neo-Confucianism. He held that the parent-child relationship should be based on both parties, not only controlled by the father. He said: "Parents could not reasonably expect filial behavior from their sons and daughters unless they in their turn, cherished, educated and set them a good example."[7] According to him, the anxieties caused by childbirth and other problems during infancy do not excuse parents from the duties. Parents should not have absolute parental authority. He argued that some behavior based on the Confucian filial piety leads not only to misery, but also hypocrisy. The Confucian filial piety produced "gentleman" who appeared moral on the outside, but was not truly moral. The act of living up to such ludicrous standards led men "...to value only the appearance of goodness, not goodness itself."⁸ He proposed a kind of filial piety, which would be maintained without a family hierarchy. The relationship between the parents and the children should be based on the natural and spontaneous affection. Ideal filial conduct should be considered to lie in the natural desire of children to rejoice the hearts of their parents. For him, filial piety was instinctive—something which should and would come naturally. In fact, his filial piety can be found in the ancient Confucianism. He also criticized the relationship between husband and wife, built on the doctrine of *meibun*. Like that of parents and children, the relationship between the husband and wife had also been based on preponderance of power. According to the Confucian canon, it was solely the duty of the wife to maintain harmony in the relationship, regardless of how her husband treated her. The wife could not argue with or disobey her husband. For him, a woman should regard her husband as Heaven was almost too ridiculous to deserve serious criticism. He attacked the Chinese tradition of keeping concubines. He said: "If a man has the right to keep two women, there can be no reason why a woman should not possess two men."⁹

## "All Men Are Created Equal" in the United States Versus All Men Are Born Equal in the Ancient Confucianism¹⁰

When we examine the sages – both the earlier and later – their principles are found to be the same.
Mencius (8: 1)

The essence of Fukuzawa's doctrines is that all humans are equal in birth. Nevertheless, it should be noted that his expression "Heaven never created a man above another or a man below another" is neither purely Western nor purely Confucian. To see possible sources of Fukuzawa's idea about equality, we examine equality in the United States and the ancient Confucianism.

American social consensus is built on the belief in freedom and equality. The core of this belief is reflected in *The American Declaration of Independence* in 1776: "We hold these truths to be self-evident, that all men are created equal, that they are endowed by their Creator with certain unalienable Rights, that among these are Life, Liberty and the pursuit of Happiness. That to secure these rights, Governments are instituted among Men, deriving their just powers from the content of the governed. That whenever any form of Government becomes destructive of these ends, it is the Right of the People to alter or to abolish it, and to institute new Government, laying its foundation on such principles and organizing its powers in such form, as to them shall seem most likely to effect their Safety and Happiness." Fukuzawa's most famous saying: "Heaven never created a man above another or a man below another" is said to origin from "all men are created equal". Nevertheless, Fukuzawa did not embody a "concrete" God to symbolize his belief. Instead, an abstract (and necessarily ambiguous) concept of "Heaven" incarnates his belief. Fukuzawa never believed any religion.

The principle of just government that "all men are created equal" underlies that all human beings possess inherent worth and dignity. It should be remarked that by "All men are created equal", Thomas Jefferson (1743-1826) did not mean that human beings were equal in all respects. By equality, he meant fundamentally political equality. He believed that no man is born to being used arbitrarily by another man; equality is a universal principle and political equality can only be effective in a republic where the citizens actually participate. The dominant opinion of the United States was articulated by John Adams, the first Vice President (1789-1797) and second President (1797-1801) of the United States, as follows: "That all men have one common nature, is a principle that will now universally prevail, and equal rights and equal duties will in a just sense, I hope, be inferred from it. But equal ranks and equal property can never be inferred from it, any more than equal understanding, agility, vigor or beauty. Equal laws are all that can ever be derived from human equality."[11] Fukuzawa held a similar rational view on distribution.

In the ancient Confucianism, the ideal of man is the sage; everyone can become sage, not through birth or power, but through self-improvement and virtue. Except the imperial family, no one's social status was determined at birth. As the Chinese Confucianism justifies rebellions against the emperor if he becomes incapable of delivering benevolence to the people, even the emperor cannot be inherited, at least, in theory. In Japan, the Confucian ideal that one's social status had to be earned by oneself had never been practiced until the Meiji Restoration. As shown in Zhang[12], Japan's Westernization was to accept the traditional Chinese practice of determining one's merits and position through efforts and knowledge and China's socialist practice was to deny this traditional Confucian practice.

In the ancient Confucianism, all men are born naturally equal. "In good years", described Mencius (11: 7), "the children of the people are most of them good, while in bad years the most of them abandon themselves to evil. It is not owing to their natural powers conferred by Heaven that they are thus different. The abandonment is owing to the circumstances through which they allow their minds to be ensnared and drowned in evil.... The sage and we are the same in kind." One is called decent human being because of one's exalted accumulation of virtue rather than exalted social status. "If a person cultivates his will and sense of purpose," explicated Hsün Tzu (2: 5), "he can take more pride in them than in riches and eminence. If he gives due weight to the Way and what is congruent with it, he will have slight regard for kings and dukes. Absorbed in the examination of his inner self, he will scorn mere external things. A tradition expresses this: The gentleman works external things; the petty man works for external things. Do whatever causes the mind to be serene though it gives the body toil, and whatever causes one's sense for what is right to develop, though it diminishes the concern for profit."

When being asked about what is that makes a man human? Hsün Tzu (5: 9) replied, "I say that it lies in his ability to draw boundaries....Even though wild animals have parents and offspring, there is no natural affection between them as between father and son, and though there are male and female of the species, there is no proper separation of sexes. Hence, the proper way of Man lies in nothing other than his ability to draw boundaries." One is entitled the gentleman only if one lives up to the high moral standards, regardless of whether one was is noble or base by birth. Hsün Tzu (1: 3) averred that "The gentleman by birth is not different from other men; he is just good at employing external things." Hsün Tzu (1: 5) also remarked: "The coming of honor or disgrace must be a reflection of one's inner power." Hsün Tzu (10: 12) argued: "The ancient Kings and sages knew that if, in creating the position of ruler and superior, they did not refine and adorn him, he would prove inadequate to the task of unifying the people; that if he were not made rich and generous, he would be inadequate to act as the pitch pipe for his subordinates; and if he were not made majestic and powerful, he would prove inadequate to proscribe the violent and overcome the cruel....They caused the various classes of people of the world to realize that what they desired and longed for was to be found with them, and this is why their incentives work. They caused them to know that what they dreaded and feared lay with them, and this is the reason their penalties inspired awe. When incentives work and penalties inspire awe, promotion of the worthy can be effected, retirement of the unworthy accomplished, and giving office to the more able and the less able according to their ability can succeed....Goods and commodities will come as easily as water bubbling from an inexhaustible spring." With regard to the principles of a king, Hsün Tzu (9: 15) instructed: "Those lacking inner power shall be without honored status, those without ability shall be without office, those who lack accomplishment shall go unrewarded, and those who do not transgress shall not be rebuked. In the loyal court, none shall occupy positions out of mere good fortune. Among the people, none shall gain a living by mere good fortune."[13]

One of the ancient Confucian tenets is that social position is arranged according to the moral attainment, merits, practical abilities, and education rather than birth. This principle is stated by Hsün Tzu (9:

1) as follows: "Although they be the descendants of kings and dukes or knights and grand officers, if they are incapable of devotedly observing the requirements of ritual and moral principles, they should be relegated to the position of commoners. Although they be the descendants of commoners, if they accumulate culture and study, rectify their character and conduct, and are capable of devotedly observing the requirements of ritual principles and justice, they should be brought to the ranks of a prime minister, knight, or grand officer." (The ancient Confucianism does not employ a 'Creator' to justify natural equality among men. 'Men are born equal' is an essential value in the ancient Confucianism.) According to Mencius (11: 6): "It is said in the Book of Poetry: 'Heaven in producing mankind, gave them their various facilities and relations with their specific laws. These are the invariable rules of nature for all to hold." Nevertheless, this does not mean that men should have equal ranks and equal property. Hsün Tzu advocated the necessity for social inequalities: "Where the classes of society are equally ranked, there is no proper arrangement of society; where authority is evenly distributed, there is no unity; and where everyone is of like status, none would be willing to serve the other.... Two men of equal eminence cannot attain each other; two men of the same low status cannot command each other – such is the norm of Heaven. When power and positions are equally distributed and likes and dislikes are identical, and material goods are inadequate to satisfy all, there is certain to become contention. Such contention is bound to produce civil disorder, and this disorder will result in poverty.... There is equality insofar as they are not equal." When being inquired about governing, Hsün Tzu (9: 1) replied: "Promote the worthy and capable without regard to seniority; dismiss the unfit and incapable without hesitation; execute the principal evildoers without trying first to instruct them; and transform the common lot men without trying first to rectify them." There is a consistent emphasis on promoting capable men to important position for the benefit of society in Confucianism. "If men of virtue and ability be not confided in," argued Mencius (14: 13), "a state will become empty and void. Without the rules of propriety and distinctions of right, the high and the low will be thrown

into confusion. Without the great principles of government and their various business,—there will not be wealth sufficient for the expenditure."

In the ancient Confucianism, all individuals are in some fundamental sense alike and no person possesses greater intrinsic worth than another. The Confucian principles based on natural equality of men don't have conflicts with democratic principles such as popular sovereignty, the right of the people to choose and hold accountable those who rule them, and the inalienable nature of human rights in an essential sense. This belief in the equal worth of all human beings also underlies profound convergence between Confucian and Western civilizations. This convergence was well recognized by Fukuzawa. What makes him different from other Confucianists of the classical learning in Japan is that he fully recognized that it is not the sages' abstract principles but the public opinion that determines the process of civilization. He had "proficiently" adapted these sages' principles according to the mainstreams of the global civilization.

## Fukuzawa's Spirit of Independence and Confucian Self-Cultivation

In *Gakumon no Susume*, he argued that the spirit of civilization is the spirit of independence among people. He viewed that civilization composes not only its outward manifestations. Law, schools, industries, the army, and the navy are all outward manifestations of the civilization. It is not difficult to establish outward manifestations because most of them can even be purchased with money. What is most important is something invisible. It cannot be seen, cannot be heard, and cannot be sold or bought. Nevertheless, when it exists among the citizens of a country, its power is strongly felt. Moreover, without it, the army or any other outward manifestations would become meaningless. This is the spirit of a civilization. This spirit is the most important factor for creating and maintaining a civilization. "What is it then?", he asked, "it is the spirit of independence among men!"[14]

In *Gakumon no Susume*, Fukuzawa compared Oriental Confucianism with Western civilization. He found what was possessed by the latter and was lacking in the former were: (1) mathematics and (2) the spirit of independence. For him, independence was a main character of Western civilization. He advocated cultivating the individual spirit of independence. On the basis of Mill's idea that "independence of a nation grows out of the independent spirit of its people", he argued that every Japanese establishes his own independence, and then Japan would be independent. In 1870 he pointed out: "Let each person accomplish his own dependence, then each family will be independent. When each family is independent, the clan will be independent. When each clan is independent, the nation itself will be secure in its independence."[15] He criticized Confucian civilizations for lacking of the spirit of independence. According to him, Confucian learning that identifies hierarchical social order as a reflection of the immutable natural order of the heavenly body imbeds a dependent and servile spirit in Japanese people. Confucianism made people to cultivate a docile and obedient attitude to power. He characterized Japanese civilization as a "preponderance of power", which exists in almost all social relations, such as relations between teacher and pupil, master and servant, rich and poor, high and low, and man and woman. This Japanese spirit led Japanese people to the apathy towards nationwide affairs. The Confucian learning also curbed the rise of commerce and manufacturing by creating distain for the pursuit of individual benefit. He observed that the Confucian teachings…"are carefully to teach children filial piety, but make no mention at all of the duties of parents. They insist that children labor for the sake of their elders, yet demand of the elders absolutely no return for their labors."[16] Blacker described: "the more querulous, exacting, unreasonable and cruel the parents were, the greater would be the merit acquired by children in behaving with the uncritical and uncomplaining meekness which was the outstanding characteristics of filial piety."[17] These unreasonable and cruel relations existed not only between the parents and children, but also among any human relation. Although he advocated the spirit of independence, he warned against behavior without sense of morality.

"The boundary between freedom and waywardness lies in whether or not one infringes on others.…One person's licentiousness will become the temptation of many, causing the general generation of the society and the disruption of education."[18]

He perceived a positive co-relationship between personal freedom and national power. Personal freedom and rights were considered as an effective means to achieve and expand national power; and national power was to create and maintain environment of personal freedom. He encouraged Japanese people to cultivate a sense of self-respect, rights, and duties. If they were not properly educated, Japanese commoners would grovel before foreign colonial masters just as they had groveled before Tokugawa feudal lords. After the Meiji Restoration of 1868, he came to believe that his mission in life was to educate his countrymen, basing on the principles of Western civilization. He held that Japan was weak and backward because its culture did not develop science and lacked the spirit of independence. To civilize Japan, it was necessary to inculcate science and cultivate the spirit of independence. He believed that by doing these, Japan would soon grow in power and wealth so as to rival Great Britain and be secure from any threat of Western attack and exploitation. In *Gakumon no Susume*, Fukuzawa advocated his principle, "national independence through personal independence." Through personal independence, an individual does not have to depend on the strength of another. With such a self-determining social morality, Fukuzawa hoped to instill a sense of personal strength among the people of Japan, and through that personal strength, build a nation to rival all others.

It is not difficult to demonstrate that Fukuzawa's spirit of independence is congenial with the concept of self-cultivation in the ancient Confucianism. The ancient Confucianism does advocate the spirit of independence as a component of filial piety. In *The Classical of Filial Piety*, Confucius said: "Therefore, in case an unrighteous conduct is contemplated, a son must in no way refrain from remonstrating with his father, nor a minister from remonstrating with his sovereignty. So remonstrance is needed whenever there is a contemplated unrighteous conduct. How can blind obedience of a son to every command of his father to be regarded as filial piety?"[19] According to the ancient Confucianism, the basis of society is individual's cultivation with knowledge and free spirit.

## Fair Reciprocity in Confucianism[20] and Fukuzawa's Principle of Equality

Fukuzawa held that human relations should be built on the principle of equality. This principle can also be found in symmetry relations as fair reciprocity in the ancient Confucianism.

China was a country of "united states" as contemporary China was once composed of many states with different cultures. The territory to where "Zhongguo" (the Chinese name for China) originally refers is still uncertain – contemporarily, it simply includes the "legal territory" of China. Chinese tradition does not believe that emperor (family) is entitled to rule by birth. Any emperor should earn his title by showing that he was able to take care of affairs of the country. If he was not qualified, the people had the right to rebel. This value provided strong incentives for ambitious men to rebel when the country was not well organized. Also because of this tradition, Chinese people accepted any ruler—even if he had obtained power through cruel forces—who would "well behave" after he won the throne. "Both the Zhou and Han dynasties", Lu Xun recorded, "had aggressive rulers, yet the Chinese sang their praise and welcomed them. They even praised the rulers of the Yuan and Qing dynasties who had come from the north. So long as the invasion was able to pacify the country and safeguard men's lives, it was the Kingly Way for which the Chinese longed."[21]

When being asked whether there was one word, which might serve as a rule of practice for all one's life, Confucius (15: 24) replied: "Is not reciprocity such a word? What you do not want done to yourself, do not do to others." Reciprocity is the key concept in the construction of social relations in Confucianism.[22] (The Confucian hierarchy is symmetry in the sense that the inferior obeys the superior (under the condition that the superior is benevolent) and the superior cares the inferior. In particular, if the superior is not benevolent, the inferior will leave the country or defy the order of the superior.) Confucius (15: 36) set up the following ultimate principle of reciprocity: "Let every man consider virtue as what devolves on himself. He may not yield the performance of it even to his teacher." When being asked what he thought of the principle that injury should be recompensed with kindness, Confucius (14: 34) answered: "With what then will you recompense kindness? Recompense injury with justice, and recompense kindness with kindness."

The Confucian hierarchy is not characterized by blind submission. In the Confucian tradition, wife is deferential to husband; but she also should reaffirm and remind her husband of the duty of mutual love and caring. Following the superiority but no blind obeying is repeatedly emphasized by Confucian doctrines. The entitlement of father is not only biological, but also social. If father does not behave properly, he simply loses the entitlement in the dutiful sense. Confucius (4: 18) never asked young people to blindly obey their parents: "In serving his parents, a son may remonstrate with them, but gently; when he sees that they do not incline to follow his advice, he shows an increased degree of reverence, but does not abandon his purpose." Confucius (12: 11) asserted: "There is government, when the prince is prince, and the minister is minister; when the father is father, and the son is son." He held that the first thing in administering the government is to rectify the names. "If names be not correct," Confucius (13: 3) pointed out: "If language be not in accordance with the truth of things, affairs cannot be carried on to success. When affairs cannot be carried on to success, proprieties, and music will not flourish. When proprieties and music do not flourish, punishments will not be properly awarded. When punishments are not properly awarded, the people do not know how to move hand or foot. Therefore, a superior man considers it necessary that the names he uses may be spoken appropriately, and also that what he speaks may be carried out appropriately." Mencius (12: 3) portrayed the Confucian obedience in the following way: "When the parents' fault was great, not to have murmured on account of it would have increased the want of natural affection. Where the parent's fault was small, to have murmured on account of it would have been to act like water which frets and foams about a stone that interrupts its course. To increase the want of natural affection would have been unfilial, and to fret and foam in such a manner would also have been unfilial." According to Mencius (8: 3): "When the prince regards his ministers as his hands and feet, his ministers regard their prince as their belly and heart; when he regards them as his dogs and horses, they regard him as any other man; when he regards them as the ground or as grass, they regard him as a robber and an enemy."

The trust among men in Confucianism is built on reciprocity. Hsün Tzu (9: 4) described what is the fair reciprocity between the ruler and the ruled: "If the lord of men desires to be secure, no policy is as good as evenhanded government and love of the people. If he desires glory, none is as good as exalting ritual principles and treating scholars with strict observance of forms of respect. If he desires to establish his fame and meritorious accomplishments, none is as good as advancing the worthy and bringing the capable into one's service." According to Mencius (3: 4), "Benevolence brings glory to a prince, and the opposite of it brings disgrace. For the princes of the present day to hate disgrace and yet live complacently doing what is not benevolent, is like hating moisture and yet living in a low situation. If a prince hates disgrace, the best course for him to pursuer, is to esteem virtue and honor virtuous scholars, giving the worthiest among them places of dignity, and the able offices of trust....Let him clearly digest the principles of his government with legal sanctions, and then even great kingdoms will be constrained to stand in awe of him."

In an open international environment, a practical way to judge a government is through people's feet. Confucius observed: "Good government obtains when those who are near made happy, and those

近者悦,远者来

61

who are far off are attracted." In an open society, choice through feet is a way to enforce freedom. Hsün Tzu (2: 6) argued: "If your deportment is respectful and reverent, your heart loyal and faithful, if you use only those methods sanctioned by ritual principles and moral duty, and if your emotional disposition is one of love and humanity, then though you travel throughout the empire, and though you find yourself reduced to living among the barbarians, everyone would consider you to be an honorable person. If you strive to be the first to undertake toilsome and bitter tasks and can leave pleasant and rewarding tasks to others, if you are proper, diligent, sincere, and trustworthy, if you take responsibility and oversee it meticulously, then wherever you travel in the civilized world and though you find yourself reduced with the barbarians, everyone would be willing to entrust with official duties." According to the Confucian standard, merely by looking at the direction and human capital of immigrants, one judges that the United States is far more well-governed than contemporary China.

## Stages of Society in Confucianism and Fukuzawa's Stages of Civilizations

文明 开化

Fukuzawa was the first to use "civilization" (*bunmei kaika*) in Japanese in *Seiyo Jijo*. The term referred to two related but different programs. The former is the goal of universal civilizations built by European philosophers and theorists. In other words, it is related to the ideal(s). The latter was pragmatic. In particular, it is concerned with the actual goals of development in guarding the country. By *bunmei kaika*, Fukuzawa implied not only that enlightenment lay on the side of what was Western but also that Japan's past was to be cast into the obscurity of shadows. Howland observes that "[T]he compound expression *bunmei kaika* was not completely foreign to Fukuzawa's educated contemporaries....Fukuzawa was the most prominent advocate of *bunmei kaika* as a universal civilization."[23]

Before the *Gakumon no Susume* was completed as a series of pamphlets, he also set to construct his major work, *Bunmeiron no*

*Gairyaku.* His ideas in the book were greatly influenced by two European works: Francio Guizot's *History of Civilization in Europe* (translated into English in 1837) and Henry Thomsa Buckle's *History of Civilization in England* of 1868. From these sources, he was able to appreciate the essence of Western civilization and establish a system (criterion) to criticize the solitary dominant system of hierarchy and passivity prevalent in Asian civilizations. He made great efforts to convince Japanese people that Japan must learn from the Western civilization for the national survival.

He held that as civilization progresses, society shows an increasing diversity of opinion and complexity of organization. This diversity is not merely an incidental characteristic of civilization, it is a necessity of its progress. Society is improved because more new ideas and opinions are created and applied. More opinions would emerge from 'interactions' of diverse ideas and opinions. Society becomes more civilized because better ideas would be created and applied than traditional ideas. This dynamics thus enables society to advance a step higher up in the ladder. If society wants to become highly civilized, it must allow a wide scope for a constant flux of ideas. Accordingly, freedom of argument is necessary for stimulating influx of ideas. As society progresses, new ideas would replace those ideas, which have been accepted by society as "fixed" and the old opinions would become useless. It is thus wrong to believe that what are good and bad are invariant with regard to time and circumstances. As society progresses, no set of ethical ideas could be maintained from one generation to the next. For Fukuzawa, "This did not imply that there was no value which could be accounted constant, true and unchanging. Such values certainly existed, but they were knowable by man only in its perfect state, at the end of the long process of progress."[24] For him, in reality what are called good or bad, right or wrong, should be adapted to its own stage of progress. Fukuzawa argued that "It was because they were guilty of precisely this confusion that the teachings of the Confucian moralists were so pernicious."[25]

In *Seiyo Jijo*, he introduced the nineteenth-century theory of social progress from savage to half-civilized to fully civilized stages. He held that a society should pass certain stages from its barbarian state to civilized one. He called each stage of social evolution or progresses as the stages of civilization. In the early stage dwellings and supplies of food are unstable and man is not able to control his conditions. He called this state as the stage of primitive man. In the next stage, which called the stage of the semi-developed stage, as agriculture has been started on a large scale, daily necessities are no more lacking. In this stage, men build houses, organize communities, and create the semblance of a state, even though men still have many defects. Though literature flourishes and men are adept at imitative craftsmanship, few people are able to devote themselves to practical studies. The society knows how to cultivate the old, but does not know how to improve the old and develop new things. Fixed human rules still control interrelations in the society. Although people are slaves of these rules, they don't alter those rules. In this stage, civilization does not yet achieve its perfection. In the next stage, men subsume the things of the universe within a general structure, even though they are not bound by the structure. People cultivate their own virtue, accumulate their own knowledge, enjoy free play and do not adhere to old customs blindly. They act freely and do not depend upon the arbitrary favors of others. They don't rest with small things but plan great accomplishments for the future and devote themselves to their realization. Their business ventures prosper day by day to increase the sources of human welfare. This modern stage of civilization is a leap far beyond the primitive or semi-developed stages.

For Fukuzawa, the concept *bunmei kaika* is not absolute but a relative one. "When we are talking about civilization in the world today," he classified, "the nations of Europe and the United States of America are the most highly civilized, while the Asian countries, such as Turkey, China, and Japan, may be called semi-developed countries, and Africa and Australia are to be counted as still primitive lands."[26] He held that the situation in semi-developed or primitive countries was harmful in the sense that when people with some intelligence in those countries·began to realize the undesirable situations or states of their own societies, they did not tend to learn hard enough from the civilized ones. He held that it was "incidental" that the new civilization had first been achieved in Europe. He did not perceive that the West was necessarily going to maintain its lead. For instance, he did not hold that high civilization could be maintained in a society where people pursue private interests at the expense of public welfare. He admitted that irrespective of all its shortcomings, European civilization was far more advanced than Japanese civilization. For him, Japan and China were semi-civilized and the distance between East and West was great. He believed that if it cultivates personal intelligence and morality, accumulates collective knowledge and makes mental advancement, keeps society in order, believes in progress, and is endowed with the spirit of independence, any society can attain civilization. To catch up with the West, Japan had to not only purchase arms, machinery and introduce "external" social and economic structures, but also cultivate the virtue and accumulate knowledge of the entire country. "To bolster people's heart …", he argues in *Bunmeiron no Gairyaku*, "there is one thing: namely, to establish our goal and advance toward civilization....The way in which to preserve this independence cannot be sought anywhere except in civilization."[27]

As our interest is to relate Fukuzawa to the essence of the ancient Confucianism, it is important to note "stages of civilization" is also perceived in the ancient Confucianism. But ancient Chinese did not believe a linear progress of civilization – the *I-Ching* does not hint this possibility for human society. According the vision of *I-Ching*, human society does not "state" at a so-called perfect state forever. Confucius' highest social ideal is of the stage of Great Principle. According to Confucius, at this stage of social evolution, the system works on the principles of universal and undifferentiated love. There is no private property, no idle class, and no private inheritance. Everyone makes his best efforts not for himself alone but also for the good of the general public. Society takes care of everyone, irrespective of age, sex or any social positions, under a perfect system. There is no national state, no war, no need of defense, no military or scheming men. The people choose men of talents, virtue and ability. The people themselves are the sovereign. There are no social ties by marriage, no relation between father and son or between brothers. People are tied by friendship and classified by age, sex or health. Each has natural love towards others. There is no artificial rites and justice. In the ancient Confucianism,[28] this golden age is described as follows

When the Great Principle prevails, the whole world becomes a republic; they elect men of talents, virtue, and ability; they talk about sincere agreement, and cultivate universal peace. Thus men do not regard, as their parents only as parents, not treat as their children only their own children. A competent provision is secured for the aged to their death, employment for the middle-aged, and the means of growing up to the young. The widowers, widows, orphans, childless men, and those who are disabled by disease, are all sufficiently maintained. Each man has his rights, and each woman her individuality safe-guarded. They produce wealth, disliking that it should be thrown away upon the ground, but not wishing to keep it for their own gratification. Disliking idleness, they labor, but not alone with a view to their own advantage. In this way selfish schemings are repressed and find no way to rise. Robbers, filches and rebellious traitors do not exit. Hence the outer doors remain open, and are not shut. This is the stage of what I call the Great Similarity.

## The Unbroken Imperial Line Justified by Fukuzawa and Kingship in the Ancient Confucianism

The brilliant palace appropriate to the emperors. If your Majesty wished to practice the true Royal government, then do not pull it down.
Mencius (371-289 BC)

Irrespective of its long history, the concept of a people as a "nation" that participated actively in the affairs of a "state" was unknown in

Japan. One of important issues in Japan's Westernization is the position of the emperor when the Western concept of "nation" was introduced. In an effort to unite the Japanese nation in response to the Western challenge, the Meiji leaders created a civic ideology centered around the emperor. The Meiji Restoration "restored" the emperor to power, but the emperor did not rule directly. Although he wielded no political power, the emperor had long been viewed as a symbol of Japanese culture and historical continuity. The emperor was the head of the Shinto religion, Japan's native religion. Among other beliefs, Shinto holds that the emperor is descended from the sun goddess and the gods who created Japan and therefore is semidivine. The Meiji reformers brought the emperor and Shinto to national prominence. By associating Shinto with the imperial line, which reached back into legendary times, Japan had not only the oldest ruling house in the world, but a powerful symbol of age-old national unity. The emperor was expected to accept the advice of the group that had overthrown the shogun, and it was from this group that a small number of ambitious, able, and patriotic young men from the lower ranks of the *samurai* emerged to take control and establish the new political system. At first, their only strength was that the emperor accepted their advice and several powerful feudal domains provided military support. They moved quickly, however, to build their own military and economic control. By July 1869 the feudal lords had been requested to give up their domains, and in 1871 these domains were abolished and transformed into prefectures of a unified central state. The feudal lords and the *samurai* class were offered a yearly stipend, which was later changed to a one-time payment in government bonds. The *samurai* lost their class privileges, when the government declared all classes to be equal. By 1876 the government banned the wearing of the *samurai*'s swords; the former *samurai* cut off their top knots in favor of Western-style haircuts and took up jobs in business and the professions. The armies of each domain were disbanded, and a national army based on universal conscription was created in 1872, requiring three years' military service from all men, *samurai* and commoner alike. A national land tax system was established that required payment in money instead of rice, which allowed the government to stabilize the national budget. This gave the government to build up the strength of the nation.

It is necessary to justify the existence of the imperial line when social and economic conditions were to be changed. Fukuzawa provided the theoretical foundation for the continuation of the imperial line. In the ancient Confucianism, the meaningful social symbol is not power itself but virtue and fairness. "What *The Great Learning* teaches is to illustrate illustrious virtue; to improve welfare of the people; and to rest in perfect benevolence. The point where to rest being known, the object of pursuit is then determined; and then, a stable social environment may be attained. To that stability there will succeed a tranquil repose. In that repose there may be careful deliberation, and that deliberation will be followed by the attainment of the desired end."[29] As shown late on, Fukuzawa applied this ancient Confucian principle to justify the continuation of the imperial line when Japan was rapidly westernizing.

The word, *kokutai* (nationality), was invented by Aizawa Seishisai, one of the most famous scholars of Mito Learning.[30] The *kokutai* was originally connected with the myth of Amaterasu and her descent in the text of Aizawa.[31] The central idea of Aizawa's ideological strategy is '*ten*' (heaven), which is originally terminology from Confucianism. Aizawa transformed its meaning and applies this word to the myth of the ancestors of the emperor (*tenno*) and the unbroken imperial line. In the chapter titled Nationality in *New Theses,* Aizawa wrote: "In antiquity, the Heavenly Progenitress, Amaterasu, set down the precepts on which to base this nation....All of Her achievements were the work of Heaven itself." Then, Aizawa insisted on the inviolable righteousness of the imperial line of Amaterasu. Aizawa held that essentials for government were ancestor worship and the edification of people by rites and music; this accordance of religious ritual, government and edification was Japanese nationality. In 1875, Fukuzawa used this word in his *Bunmeiron no Gairyaku* but gave it a new meaning. He translated the word "nationality" in John Stuart

Mill's *Representative Government* as *kokutai'*. He regarded the common memory of a nation as the core of *kokutai*. But in *Brief Comments on Current Affairs* (*Jiji Shogen*) published in 1881, he changed his opinion. He criticized Christianity, and accepted the myth of the unbroken imperial line.[32] He was critical of the traditional idea of nationality. In *Bunmeiron no Gairyaku*, he argued: "*Kokutai* means the state of a nation where people are independent from others, enjoy and grieve together, discriminate against other people in favor of their own and govern themselves under their own government." For him, *kokutai* did not imply the *bakufu* regime and the unbroken imperial line. He tried to identify *kokutai* through differentiating between 'Self' and 'Others'. It was from Mill that he learned the idea of nationality, which he translated as *kokutai*. According to Mill, nationality may have many origins such as race, religion, language, geography, but the strongest factor is a history by which people have the same memory about their nation.

Fukuzawa did not explicitly reject the traditional idea of the myth of the unbroken imperial line, which had been important for Japanese intellectuals to show the nation's supremacy. As he believed that the strongest factor for solidifying nationality was the same memory about their nation, he would use the national memory to strengthen patriotism. In 1882 he wrote a comment on an edict issued by the government. In his comment entitled '*Duties of Shinto Priests*', he maintained that the duties of Shinto priests were to foster the common historical memory of the nation and to enforce national strength by giving lectures about Japanese history. He wrote: "Never being invaded by the foreigners since the founding of the nation, we Japanese have maintained the imperial line."[33] After he had found the concept of national memory and identified the common national memory, he could "Westernize" the myth of the unbroken imperial line from Mito Learning and National Learning. One week after he published *Duties of Shinto Priests*, he published a famous article entitled *Imperial Family* (*Teishitu Ron*). He theorized that the imperial family should be situated outside politics. The imperial family was justified as national symbol to nationally integrating the people. In *Teishitu Ron*, he claimed: "Our Imperial Family is a perfect jewel never damaged since its foundation. Under its brilliance we the people gather around it to keep the social order within, and to expand our national strength outside." [34] In *Reverence for the Emperor* (*Sonno Ron*) in 1888, he advocated that the imperial family should be neutral, and reverence for the family should be an inviolable discipline for Japanese people. He held that in the West, religion encouraged virtue and a charitable spirit, whereas in Japan, religion was confined within the precinct of a temple. Japanese people should depend on the imperial throne for a virtuous life. The function of the imperial throne was to establish a symbol for the people's loyalty, which could not be found in laws. He believed that as in business world, loyalty mattered a lot for national building. In *Teishitu Ron,* he pointed out, "Rates of pay and hours of work alone could not command the loyalty of an employee towards his employer....It was the emperor who should be the focus of this emotional side of the people's relations with the government."[35] He posited the imperial house as the non-partisan focal-point at the center of Japanese society, which would keep all the Japanese people in harmony and comfort.

He believed that the way the virtues of the Imperial Household influence the people is mystical and powerful.[36] The emperor touring the country incognito could save a person in poverty and increase the productivity of the whole province. There is an almost endless list of merits associated with the Imperial Household. The Imperial Household could be the symbol of the nation; command the spirit of soldiers of the navy and the army; supplies purposes to the devotion of these soldiers; ask for loyal children and faithful wives for raising the moral standard of the nation; encourage learning, spread education and recognize able scholars; save the arts from the brink of extinction; and increase the wealth of the nation. He opened his 1882 essay *On the Imperial Household* as follows:[37] "Among the affairs in this country, there is none weightier than the Imperial Household." By 1882, there had been a few articles published on the sovereignty issues. But some of these articles were based on the neo-Confucian and classical Japanese philosophies. For an enlightened mind, according to him, these arguments were hardly worth noticing. The other articles even lacked logic reasoning.

He held that the Imperial Household is an entity outside of the political world. The Imperial family should stand apart from and above political schemes and strives. The family should be the source of honors and rewards granted to the people by the state, but never of punishment or dishonor. He argued: "It has been my constant thought that all men living in Japan who discuss politics or who hold positions in government must not exploit the dignity and the sanctity of the Imperial Household."[38] He held that the Imperial Household is important for promoting the ideal that all people are equal. He held: "Observed from the exalted position of the Imperial Household, all the people must be regarded as equal, including the rebels and traitors. From the omnipresent benevolence, there is no difference in its blessings for all the subjects."[39] He considered that the encouragement of learning should be carried out by the Imperial Household. He believed that the country would benefit from this. He hoped: "I wrote of my wish to have the Imperial Household as the central sponsor of learning in our country. This idea also includes my wish to keep Japan's learning independent of government and politics."[40]

In the early 1883, he suggested that Tokyo needed a comprehensive city plan that would revolve around a magnificent palace's construction. At this time, officials of Tokyo's prefectural government did not seem to be aware of a comprehensive plan in city construction and had no concrete designs about urban development. They were busy with constructing waterways, gas lines, railways, and bridges in a piecemeal fashion with no overall plan. He emphasized the necessity that the government immediately paid attention to city planning. For Fukuzawa, the most urgent, large-scale, and long-term task should be to build the imperial palace, rather than construction of Tokyo harbor or election of a symbolical structure like the Capitol building in

Washington or any number of other edifices as suggested by others. The capital could then be developed around it. "Since the palace would be a permanent structure for the 'Japanese emperors whose successive reigns are coeval with Heaven and Earth,' and since a palace is 'the place where the emperor of our divine country (*waga shinshu*) conducts ceremonies of intercourse with monarchs and presidents of the myriad nations,' he stressed that every effort should be made to make the palace 'splendid and beautiful to accord with our national power.'"[41] Like what Mencius emphasized long time ago, in order to provide the symbol of virtue and righteousness, the palace should be as splendid and beautiful as possible, so far the national economic power allowed. The places, not only inner the palace, but also outside the palace, should be built splendidly. He was deeply concerned with demonstrating national power and the level of Japan's civilization. In particular, he emphasized that in an age when the entire world was connected like a house, Japan should impress foreigners with the capital and the imperial palace at its core. The construction of the palace and the capital were closely related to national prestige and international relations. He reprehended those who disapproved building a great capital city with a splendid imperial palace for financial reasons. He censured those who admired the virtues of monarchical self-sacrifice for the people and said that they simply did not understand the necessities imposed by international politics and progress. His views on the significance of the imperial place appeared in official plans for the rebuilding of the capital. He wanted to impress foreign powers. He insisted that the customs of common people's everyday lives should be kept out of view near the palace.

To relate his arguments about the role of the Imperial Household to the ancient Confucianism, we examine greatness and wealth in Confucianism.[42] Greatness and riches, if not associated with virtue and ability, were not important in Confucius' own mind. In Confucian tradition they are respectable only when they are obtained in the proper way.) Nevertheless, Confucian tradition does not devalue the importance of desires and emotions for individual life as well as for

72

society. (Confucius held that the means of satisfying desires is not to eliminate them; nor is it to diminish them; it is rather to guide them into proper channels.) The following saying of Hsün Tzu asserted this attitude towards desires: "Each doctrine of good conduct which depends upon the elimination of desires, has no way of guiding the desires, but is hampered by the presence of desire. Every doctrine of good conduct which expects the lessening of desires has no way to curb the desires but is hampered by the great number of desires." (Confucius held that man naturally desires to be great and to be rich. There is nothing wrong with desires themselves. It is wrong to employ unjust means to satisfy desires. The master related: "Riches and honors are what men desire. If they cannot be obtained in the proper way, they should not be held. Poverty and meanness are what men dislike. If they cannot be avoided in the proper way, they should not be avoided.")

Confucius held that different minds have diferent attitudes towards virtue and profit: "The mind of the superior man is conversant with righteousness; the mind of the mean man is conversant with gain." (Irrespective of his positive attitudes towards wealth and greatness, Confucius observed that it is not material wealth but virtue and personality that make one's reputation lasting. Confucius emphasized cooperation among men. Men should not strive to get the better of each other, but to promote the common welfare. In particular, a ruler's success should be measured by his ability. The benevolent ruler is not to amass wealth and power for himself, but to bring about the welfare and happiness to the people. Social symbols like wealth and position are significant in society. People should show respect to different symbols according to what they stand for. On the other hand, the doctrine of the rectification of names requires that there should be a correct correspondence between the actuality and the essence that the symbol is supposed to stand for. (In the ancient Confucianism socioeconomic symbols such as wealth and trade are not despised. If one is virtuous and talented, one should hold power, obtain riches, receive respected, and live long as well. This is to follow rather than be against the Way. This is illustrated by Confucius' following saying in

*The Doctrine of the Mean*: "Therefore having such great virtue [like Shun], it could not but be that he should obtain the throne, that he should obtain those riches, that he should obtain fame, that he should attain to his long life."

The ancient Confucianism highly values objective symbols such as official positions, wealth and educational degrees. To have power almost always means to be rich in the Confucian tradition. The association of (just) power with wealth is justified in the Confucian tradition. The ruler's wealth does not exist for the emperor to enjoy himself. Rather, he should utilize this wealth as a means to share his people's joy or sorrow. The palace stands for the significance of the emperor's duties. In the ancient Confucianism, the sole purpose of government is to improve the welfare of the people. Sustainability of government is determined by whether it delivers to people what they like (democracy is an acceptable way to aggregate preferences of miscellaneous peoples). If government does what people are against, it cannot last long. Mencius (2: 1) advised: "If your Majesty now will make pleasure a thing common to the people and yourself, the Imperial sway awaits you." Mencius (7: 8) reasoned that "There is a way to get the empire—get the people, and the empire is got. There is a way to get the people—get their hearts, and the people are got. There is a way to get their hearts;—it is simply to collect for what they like, and not to lay on them what they dislike." The following paragraph illustrates what Mencius (2: 2) meant to enjoy as the people enjoy: "The king Xuan of Qi, asked, 'was it so, that the park of King Wen contained seventy square li?' Mencius replied: 'It is so in the records.' Exclaimed the king: 'was it so large as that?' Mencius said: 'The people still looked on it as small." The king added: 'My park contains only forty square *li*, and the people still look on it as large. How is this?' The reply was: 'The park of King Wen contains seventy square lie, but the grass-cutter, and the fuel-gathers had the privilege of entrance into it; so also had the catchers of pheasants and hares. He shared it with the people, and was it not the reason that they looked on it as small? When I first arrived at the borders of your state, I required about the great prohibitory regulations, before I would venture to enter it; and I heard, that inside the border gates there was a park of forty square *li*, and that he who killed a deer in it, was held guilty of the same crime as if he had killed a man. Thus those forty square *li* are a pitfall in the middle of the kingdom. Is it not with reason that the people look upon them as large?" This is further confirmed by what Mencius (2: 4) argued: "When superiors of the people do not make enjoyment a thing common to the people and themselves, they do wrong. When a ruler rejoices in the joy of his people, they also rejoice in his joy; when he grieves at the sorrow of his people, they also grieve at his sorrow. A sympathy of joy will pervade the empire, a sympathy of sorrow will do the same – in such a state of things, it cannot be but that the ruler attain to the Imperial dignity."

If a king's wealth makes the people happy, the people would not begrudge him his wealth. It is in this sense that in the Confucian tradition the ruler's wealth is glorified. As Fukuzawa put the first priority on the safety of the nation, he emphasized the necessity of demonstrating the glory of Japan. His justification about the continuation of the imperial line is essentially consistent with the ancient Confucianism which he had read before starting the Western learning.

## Law and Duty According to Fukuzawa and the Ancient Confucianism

A man who has no laws at all is lost and guideless. A man who has laws but does not understand their meaning is timid and inconsistent. Only if a man abides by laws and the same time comprehends their wider significance and applicability can he become truly liberal and compassionate.

Hsün Tzu (298-238 BC)

According to the ancient Confucianism the most desirable social structure is one governed by virtuous men. Nevertheless, even if a society fails to produce and place virtuous men at important positions, it would not collapse if the law is still followed. Hsün Tze (6: 12) pointed out

> Though it lacks old and perfected men,
> Still it has the law,
> Yet none will even follow the law,
> For this the Great Mandate is tumbling down.

In his speech at the 358th meeting of the Mita Oratorical Society on September 24, 1898, Fukuzawa described what had been practiced in the past Japan: "the feudal lord governed his people as he pleased....Matters of prosperity and failure – even of life and death – were left entirely in the hands of their one single master."[43] (In the traditional Japan, there were no written (public) laws as even if laws existed, the government kept them as secrets and the ordinary people did not know them.) He then encouraged people to study law, using examples in daily life to illustrate the necessity of familiarizing law. He told people that this is both for protecting themselves as well as benefiting the society in large. (People are individual, also members of families and belong to nations. These associations impose upon people "natural" limits to liberty, which Fukuzawa termed "duty". (One's duty begins naturally from the most fundamental right of liberty: each man's efforts to preserve his own person.) One's duty is extended to one's family, and then to the general duties to prevent trouble for others and to obeying the law. He held that duty keeps the free individual from selfish behavior. In this way, human community would be held together both with the law and the duty.[44] Although he considered the law the pillar of society, he did not advocate freedom under law. People must cultivate a sense of duty.)

To see how his attitude towards duty is related to the ancient Confucianism, we first notice that like him (as well as Adam Smith), the ancient Confucianism holds that law is not sufficient to cultivate moral sense. The ancient Confucianism does not believe that one can easily identify some way to universal justice. "The empire, its State, and its families," according to Confucius, "may be perfectly ruled; dignities and emoluments may be declined; naked weapons may be trampled under the feet; but the course of the Mean cannot be attained to." In *The Doctrine of the Mean*, Confucius claimed: "Perfect is the virtue which is according to the Mean. Rare have they long been among the people, who could practice it!". Confucius also described that the path of the truth had not been walked in: "The knowing go beyond it, and the stupid do not come up to it." According to Confucius, the path of the Mean is rarely understood because "the men of talents and virtue go beyond it, and the worthless do not come up to it. There is no body but eats and drinks. But they are few who can distinguish flavors." In *The Doctrine of the Mean*, Confucius observed: "Men all say, 'We are wise'; but being driven forward and taken in a net, a trap, or a pitfall, they know not how to escape. Men all say, 'We are wise'; but happening to choose the course of the Mean, they are not able to keep it for a round month." Mungello observed, "Confucianism repeatedly blends morality and truths of nature in what a superficial reader of the texts might call a confusion of the two. But confusion hardly applies to the deeper understanding that Confucian philosophy has traditionally borne in relation to its Western counterparts. In Confucianism, morality is melded with the truth of the natural world and blended with the seeking of truth in an individual man. Traditionally, only a moral man was fully entitled to the description of "learned." Our tendency to scoff at this as nothing more than a mouthed ideal misses a connection that the Chinese were quite clear about and still are....The modern West has seen the rise of technical experts whose expertise is judged quite apart from their qualities as good men; perhaps this is because we have become preoccupied with external knowledge. But when we come to knowledge that involves our inner selves, a dynamic connection emerges between the kind of person we are and what we can know."[45] Fukuzawa did not miss the Confucian concept of self-cultivation and duty.

## Law for Confucius, Adam Smith and Fukuzawa

Fukuzawa's thought was influenced by Western learning. As mentioned before, he emphasized law as well as duty in maintaining social order. In the ancient Confucianism, duty is emphasized and in liberalism law is believed to be sufficient for social order. To see these differences, let us contrast the opinions on law and propriety held by Adam Smith and Confucius.[46]

Whether society should be governed through rules of justice or rules of propriety is a major difference between the Confucian and Western civilizations. By justice, Smith meant the observance of a set of legal rules by which each person's freedom is reasonably secured. He held that justice is a necessary but not a sufficient condition for the achievement of full virtue: "Systems of positive law, therefore, though they deserve the greatest authority, as the records of the sentiments of mankind in different ages and nations, yet can never be regarded as accurate systems of the rules of natural justice."[47] He suggested that the model of moral judgment, in the metaphor of the impartial spectator, establishes a hierarchy of virtues: The virtues derived from the impartial spectator are of the first order, and those derived from obligations to rules of justice are second order or lower order. Smith acknowledged that it is not entirely clear when our actions ought to be determined chiefly or entirely from the rules of justice, and in what circumstances some other sentiment or affection ought to concur.

Smith believed that people are not likely to achieve moral excellence, that they have a natural tendency to harm each other, and that society cannot flourish among those who are ready to hurt each other at all times. Still, Smith maintained that men could be made to follow rules of justice: "The regard to those general rules of conduct is what is properly called a sense of duty,...the only principle by which the bulk of mankind are capable of directing their actions."[48] This implies that first-order virtue is not, in reality, reliable among the majority of mankind. In contrast to Confucius, Smith held that society might operate well even if each individual is driven only by self-interest, without benevolence: "Society may subsist among different men, as among different merchants, from a sense of its utility, without any mutual love or affection; and though no man in it should owe any obligation, or be bound in gratitude to any other, it may still be upheld by a mercenary exchange of good offices according to an agreed valuation." And again, "Beneficence…is less essential to the existence of society than justice. Society may subsist, though not in the most comfortable state, without beneficence; but the prevalence of injustice must utterly destroy it."[49] For Smith, benevolence—the foundation of Confucius' moral philosophy—is strictly optional.

Conversely, Confucius held that social order and justice are maintained by mutual obligation in terms of virtue and ceremonies, rather than by law, since, as was discussed above, he did not believe that law would make people virtuous. Confucius maintained that ceremony should play a role analogous to that which law plays in a constitutional society. Ceremony is a means of establishing norms, by custom, and is less rigid than law. In Confucian tradition, there are two principle means for enforcing the rules of propriety. First, education to develop virtues such as loyalty, sincerity, good faith, justice, and kindness. Confucius proposed equal opportunity of education for all: "There being instruction, there will be no distinction of classes." Second, Confucian tradition created the doctrine of the rectification of names to enforce rules of propriety. Confucius thought that it is important for society to maintain the correct correspondence between social symbols (such as money, wealth, and social position) and the meanings that these symbols are supposed to signify. His argument about rectifying names is of central importance to understanding Confucianism: "If names be not correct, language is not in accordance with the truth of things,…affairs cannot be carried on to success,…proprieties and music will not flourish,…punishments will not be properly awarded, [and]…the people do not know how to move hand or foot."

Confucius and Smith also differ in their views on class. Smith emphasized birth and fortune in society, and that is an important difference between Smith's social system and Confucianism. Smith argued: "Nature has wisely judged that the distinction of ranks, the peace and order of society, would rest more securely upon the plain and palpable difference of birth and fortune, than upon the invisible and often uncertain difference of wisdom and virtue. The undistinguishing eyes of the great mob of mankind can well enough perceive the former: it is with difficulty that the nice discernment of the wise and the virtuous can sometimes distinguish the latter."[50] If order is to be maintained mainly through rules of propriety, the government has to be able to make creative and fair judgments according to different situations. In such a society, even a man born into good fortune cannot perform his duty if he is not talented and properly educated. On the other hand, if a society is run according to rules of justice, the government can administer its affairs routinely. If the government can secure people's respect and trust (birth and fortune are obviously helpful in that), it can maintain society. The government that rules by justice has less need to select talented and creative minds.

Basing his theory on passions (or sympathy) and the rules of justice, Smith concluded that it is in freedom that a harmonious and good society is created. He held that under natural force, society displays a hierarchical structure sustained by subordination. In principle, birth and fortune do not count for much in one's social positions in traditional Chinese thinking. Confucius argued that the morally preeminent ought to be entitled to high social positions. He advocated universal education and taught that diplomatic and administrative positions should go to those best qualified academically, not socially. Confucius said, "When right principles prevail in the empire, government will not be in the hands of the great officers. When right principles prevail in the empire, there will be no discussions among the common people." Non-active policy is an ideal state in Confucianism. One may see that Confucius would consider no government intervention as the most perfect state of a nation.

Confucius' attitude towards propriety may be used to illustrate some limitations of Smith's rules of justice. Rites tend to be observed consistently over time, whereas fashion clearly can change very rapidly. If society is kept in order by the rules of justice and there are no constraints by which to define propriety, people might lose the sense of what is right or wrong. On the other hand, Smith's attitude towards propriety may be used to illustrate some limitations of Confucius' rules of propriety "To act with the most perfect propriety, requires no more than that common and ordinary degree of sensibility or self-command which the most worthless of mankind are possessed of, and sometimes even that degree is not necessary."[51] A society governed by propriety would collapse, as it does not have social mechanisms to produce "capable and good citizens" in the long term.

As Zhang[52] observes, Confucius and Smith might have been influenced by differences in the historical conditions they faced rather than their moral philosophy. They have similar viewpoints with regard to benevolence, the rules of justice, and rules of propriety. Smith chose rules of justice partly because he lived in a mobile and industrializing economy, while Confucius chose rules of propriety partly because he lived in an agricultural economy with low mobility. As mentioned by Gordon[53], once medieval England was safe from foreign invasion, the concept of economic and political liberty began to become prevalent. Having suffered from foreign invasions and control, the English embraced the thought that individuals were born with rights. No one, not even the king, could take away from individuals these rights. The idea of the majesty of the law is today encapsulated in the rule of law.  Gordon deemed it "one of the most important of Western concepts, for without it the Western achievements of the 19th century would not have been possible." The law played an important role in enabling the decent ruler to control foreign lands in a civilized manner. It is not difficult to see that the traditional Confucian way of governing with propriety may not be suitable for a mobile society where multiple cultures co-exist. But Japan has successfully maintained a non-Western industrial economy, built on a concern for propriety—partly because it is not multi-cultural and has not had to contend with varied (or even conflicting) values.

## The People, the Government, and the Scholar

In antiquity, men undertook learning for the sake of self-improvement; today people undertake learning for the sake of others.
Hsün Tze (1:10)

Fukuzawa held that value does not lie in things themselves, but in the way they work. Nothing is in itself good or bad; it is only the way in which it is related to others which makes it so. Customs or ideas might be desirable in one context, but become undesirable in another. "Taken by itself", he argued, "nothing can be said to be good or bad....The doctrine of loyalty to one's master, the doctrine of Christianity, of Buddhism, of Confucianism, are neither wise nor foolish in themselves, but only in the way in which they are carried out."[54] This is similarly true for the principles of the distinction between lord and vassal and between high and low and of respect for lineage and family. These distinctions may be useful or harmful, depending on how they are used. As men have difficulties in correctly choosing among all various alternatives and greater knowledge is companied with greater diversity, according to Fukuzawa, this kind of problems would be solved with time. He believed: "Man's own nature was suited to progress because it contained within it a guiding principle in the form of a *honshin*, an original, essential nature, which was absolutely good."[55] As man possesses this original mind, man could become perfectible. The perfection of man's was the liberalization of the original mind. Once people's mind independently functions, they would spontaneously and immediately behave according to the ultimate values. Moreover, he insisted that ultimate values could not be described or defined in terms of the ordinary moral words. Concrete values such as loyalty are useful in some stages of civilization but would be discarded in late stages. Blacker observes; "his picture of the perfected man...is remarkably reminiscent of the neo-Confucian perfect man who has returned to his original good nature." [56]

He held that a nation or a society is a "gathering" of people. The element of the gathering is individual; and the purpose of the gathering is not for the sake of the gathering but for improvement of welfare – which is dependent on security and social order – of the elements. He argued that to achieve the collective goal of Japan's independence in the world, a balance of power must be achieved between government and people. He compared the nation to a human body, the health of which is maintained by internally managing external stimuli (heat, cold, pain). The nation was supposed to maintain political activity by equalizing the internal power of the government and the external power of the people. The power of the government and the power of the people are necessary to maintain a "healthy nation". He viewed Japan being backward because the government had taken upon itself the work of instructing the people in the three areas of learning, law, and commerce in an authoritarian manner.

He encouraged people to carry out their duty with the spirit of independence. They should not lose the spirit against wrongdoings of the government. In *Gakumon no Susume*, if people have something to complain against the government or officials, they should not be silent, but seek the proper ways to present the case. He said: "If the case should be in accordance with Heaven's reason and with humanity, one should fight for it even at the risk of one's life."[57] Since the common people might be unable to accumulate sufficient knowledge to judge properly what are right or wrong and the government is mainly interested in maintaining its power, it is thus the duty of the scholar to guard the path of civilization because the scholar has knowledge and the spirit of independence. If the country wants to be independent, it must maintain a balance of power. He held that to maintain the independence of the country and to regulate social and economic activities, there must be a proper balance of the power of the government within and the power of the people outside. Through his school, Keio Gijuku, and his publications, he strove to create the "middle class" who could lead the Japanese economy on the base of their intellectual forces. In his view, the growth of the middle class would bring a balance of power in the relations between the government and the people. Under the principle of division of labor, the government was entrusted to form legislations and policies for the sake of nation and the private sector would support it by their cooperation and their own initiatives.

He did not believe that the progress of civilization could be enforced by the government alone. He did not think that a nation's civilization could be initiated from above by the government or started from below by the lower classes. He held that civilization "has to start in the middle of society to indicate the path for the majority and stand side by side to indicate the path for this attempt."[58] For him, the government is necessary because people are ignorant. When people are educated and progress in civilization is achieved, people would seek their own way to civilization. But he did not believe that this ideal stage was available to Japan in the short term. He held that Japan had been oppressed under despotic governments for some thousands of years and the people had no ability to express their ideas. Under the despotic governments the people came to consider deception and artifice as necessary devices in human life. They did not feel shame about insincerity and dishonesty. He felt that there is no way to escape this evil trap and the final consequence of deepened distrust between the government and the people is inevitable. It would lead to no positive long-term consequences in promoting civilization by giving all the power to the government alone.

He argued that to promote civilization and spirit of independence, there should be a person before others as an example toward which all others may endeavor to strive. But the problem remains where to find such a person. He did not think that such a person could be found in farmers, merchants or scholars of Chinese and Japanese learning. "The only area one may hopefully find someone will be among the scholars of Western learning. And yet, there is a reason for not pinning my hopes on this group."[59] He did not trust the scholars of Western learning for the mission because although the number of these scholars had been increased, they could not carry out the mission.[60] They were either unable to understand what they had read or they did not have good faith to put the knowledge into practice. With Japanese scholars in general, He observed: "The scholars in our society are mostly cowards, and they haven't much mettle to be counted on, but their ability to decipher difficult texts is always admirable."[61] He attacked these scholars of Western learning, "These people, supposedly scholars, seem to recognize the importance of government alone and do not seem to realize even the existence of the citizenry."[62] As scholars independent of the government should play the leading role in civilizing Japan, these trained in the West could not complete the mission. According to Fukuzawa, "It is true that to promote an idea it is better to teach it than to command it; it is still better to demonstrate it than to teach it. The government, of its own nature, possesses no other function than one of authority." [63] He held that teaching and demonstrating would be performed only by private people. In particular, he considered himself as a pioneer in this direction. He considered it his own task to demonstrate with his own behaviour and actions the proper path of progress for the Japanese society. Through teaching and demonstrating, people will understand the principles of independence. Then, the people and the government will act in balance to create a country with the spirit of independence.

## On Gender Relations

Let the people be employed in the way, which is tended to secure their ease, and though they are toiled, they will not murmur.
Mencius (13:13)

"Every time I read Sensei's articles on Japanese women in *Jiji-shimpo*," it is written in a letter passed anonymously to his wife at the time of Fukuzawa's funeral, "I feel grateful that he is our real friend....With my tears, I sincerely hope that Sensei's desires shall permeate our country for ever."[64] This letter has been frequently cited because it recodes not only the feeling of the heart revealing it, but the deep appreciation and feeling of many Japanese people.

Fukuzawa was one of the first Japanese to study women's positions in society.[65] In Confucian tradition, relations between man and woman and their implications are seldom discussed. Fukuzawa pointed out that gender relations were very important but these relations had never been seriously examined in the Asian countries. [66] In traditional Japanese society, women were destined to serve and obey men, to be gentle and meek, and accomplished in household. As his father died when he was only two years old, his mother managed the family and brought up the five children. He was also greatly influenced by Mill's *The Subjection of Women* and Wayland's *Elements of Moral Science.*

He was critical of the custom of polygamy prevalent in Japan. He held that a family of one husband and one wife should be the basic form of human society as well as the basis for moral relationships. He argued that there is no reason to distinguish the relative importance or dignity of man and woman. The wife should not serve the husband as if he were a master and she a servant. Man and woman should be independent and help each other to be independent. The spirit of independence of the husband and the wife would lead to that of the family, ultimately leading to the national spirit of independence. For women to be spiritually independent, Fukuzawa believed that they must have economic independence. He believed that all girls in Japan should receive an education. In *On Japanese Women* in 1885, he advocated the importance of education for women and the improvement of their position in society.[67] Society should afford women the same rank as men, the same rights, and the same rights of ownership of property as men. Men and women are different in their body structures and the workings of their minds. When human beings are considered the masters of creation, he argued, both men and women are the masters. If a nation can no longer exist without man, it can also no longer exist without woman.

For him, marriage was a union of two independent individuals forming a cooperative union. This union, called the family, should be independent of the old unions from which they originated. One concrete suggestion he made toward the realization of equality between married couples was related to family names. When the two get married, they should discard their original family names and create a new one for the new family. For woman to be independent, he argued that she must be independent in the physical, legal, and economic fields. In Japan, over centuries social oppression had made women physically inferior to men. For women to regain heir health, they should improve their nourishment, recreation, and relaxation. Woman should have equal rights in marriage and divorce as man. He asked for equal rights for husband and wife in their ownership as well as in inheritance of the house they lived in and all other property they owned. He supported equal division of property to both sons and daughters and the necessity of work outside the home for women to earn their own incomes. He averred that the human relationships promoted by Confucianism made women miserable and caused immorality in men. He suggested a number of changes. He argued that in order to have equality within the husband-wife relationship, women had to be able to inherit and own property. Women would no longer be completely dependent on their husbands. Their husbands, thus, would be forced to show some level of respect towards them, which would, in turn help to break down the family hierarchy.⁶⁸ In *On Japanese Women* in 1885, he argued that if women get equal rights with their husbands and become independent of their husbands, women's responsibilities and worries would be increased. The increase in worry will bring about please as well. In end, women have to become active in both mind and body. Hence, the independence of women is also to benefit Japan as a nation. He argued: "To make them more active, women must be given more responsibilities and more enjoyments." ⁶⁹

In *On Morality* in 1885 he tried to convince Japanese people that Japanese men should correct their behavior. He believed that that a greater portion of Japanese men were nothing but cripples. They had no idea of the spirit of independence. He even did not believe that he was able to make these men to self-reflect. Since these men were so difficult to be reformed, he would let bygones by bygones. But in the future, in order to make men behave properly, Japanese society should suppress the wayward ways and nonchalance inherited from their warrior ancestors and also clarify the faults in Confucian teachings. He advocated three principles for Japanese society to follow in the near future: first, that young men stop imitating their predecessor's obnoxious habits; second, that if those young men are unable to resist urges, they should keep their acts as the greatest secrets of their lives; and, third, that they recognize the customs as ugly and try avoiding them. He held that if a man claims to be the lord of creation, he has to keep himself thoroughly right. But according to his observations of the "natural behavior" of human beings, he thought that it would be very difficult to lead perfectly moral lives, except perhaps for feeble and torpid men who do not have the energy or need to violate the rule and the healthy and active men, who while physically capable, are wise and brave to restrain themselves. It would be useless to expect the "average men" to refrain themselves from acts of immorality. According to him, a man sometimes does bad things because he is human; but even when one is imperfect, one should still minimize negative consequences. As point pouted by Nishikawa[70], from his arguments on women, Fukuzawa might hold too narrow a view. For example, he never advocated public activism for women. He did not examine the issue of women in the labor force (most of women worked in wretched conditions). He considered prostitution as an evil institution. Nevertheless, he held that it was a necessity for single men, especially for those who were too poor to marry. He held that the prostitute is immoral and degraded, but she was necessary for society. He was not against the prostitution of poor girls or their migration overseas, since he regarded it as preferable to starvation.

# 4

# Learning, Education and Confucian Meritocracy

Moralists and saints had done almost nothing but comments on the principles laid down by Christ and Confucius....But in scientific knowledge, we know a hundred things where the ancients knew one.
Fukuzawa[1]

There was perhaps no single sentence so powerful in influencing Japanese Westernization as Fukuzawa's famous saying: "Heaven does not create some people above or below others." The statement denied the traditional belief that the upper class was born to rule. For him, the traditional feudal system was a disease that Japan inherited from the ancient ancestors. It denies the entire socioeconomic structure of traditional Japanese society as well as Japanese Confucianism. His saying singled the start of a new system of beliefs.

As pointed out by Zhang[2], a main merit of the Meiji Restoration of 1868 and the establishment of the new bureaucratic state is a long-delayed realization of Confucian meritocracy in Japanese civilization. To change one's social status by learning had been practiced long time in China before the Meiji Restoration, even though this was almost unthinkable when Fukuzawa was born in Japan. Japanese modernization is to practice Chinese tradition in the sense that people who manage the country are mainly chosen by merit. He believed that people are born neither exalted nor base, or neither rich nor poor. He held that those who work hard at their studies and learn much should become exalted and rich, while those who are ignorant should become base and poor. This later became the Meiji government's ideology. In *Gakumon no Susume*, he argued for equality of people and free choice of professions and emphasized education: "In order to understand the logic of things, one must be literate. This is the reason for the urgent need for education."[3] He advocated equal opportunities for all people in education. The equality in education enables the best and brightest, no matter what station in life they were born into, to assume positions of power and influence for the betterment of a society as a whole.

He asked Japan to switch from the Japanese Confucian practice of social immobility to the Chinese Confucian practice of determining one's social positions through learning and efforts, like in the traditional China,[4] with the emperor as exception. In *On Morality* in 1885, he argued that the national power lies at whether its people are weak or strong. To build a strong Japan, the nation should be virtuous and educated, which are measured by virtuous behavior of people and intellectuals. He held that education was the essence for civilizing Japan and every man could benefit from at least a rudimentary education. Only when the Japanese people were taught to stand independently could the Japanese nation hope to be free of the influence of Western powers.

## Some Western Thinkers' and Fukuzawa's Criticisms Against Confucianism

Fukuzawa claimed himself to be a believer in Confucianism. But he fiercely attacked Confucianism. This book demonstrates that as far as the basic principles are concerned, Fukuzawa is Confucian; but as far as concrete values and institutions he supported, he is westernized. In fact, the intellectual attitudes toward Confucianism were changed in

Europe over time. In the age of the enlightenment, European thinkers showed admiration of Chinese culture, in particular, Confucianism. But as Europe had experienced industrialization, they began to despise Chinese culture and criticize Confucianism. In particular, during the Fukuzawa lifetime, American thinkers had almost no positive attitude towards anything Chinese because when American thinkers started constructing socioeconomic thought based on the European tradition, European thinkers had already had used Chinese civilization as the symbol of social stagnation.

Although the European intellectuals were familiar with some aspects of Chinese culture as early as the 13th century after Marco Polo's expedition to China, a main step had not been taken until the 16th century when the Europeans began to rapidly expand consciousness, interest and power. In the 16th century cultural exchange between Europe and China was conducted through missionary activities. The role played by Matteo Ricchi (1552-1610) of Mazzarino in Italy was historically important. He translated the Confucian Four Books into Italian. It was the first Western language version of the Confucian works. A Latin version of three, *The Great Learning*, *The Mean* and *The Analects* of the Four Books by Ignatius de Costa, Prosper Intorcenta, and Philippus Couplet was published in the name of the *Confucius Sinarum Philosophus* in Paris in 1687. In the 17th century the main focus on China was concentrated on the Confucian doctrines. Scant attention was paid to other Chinese classics and their translation into Western languages began only toward the end of the 19th and the beginning of the 20th century.

Gottfried Wilhelm Leibniz, born at Leipzig in Saxony on 23 June 1646, is one of the greatest thinkers of Western civilization. He was one of the foremost mathematicians of his time and a philosopher of enduring fame. Things Chinese, such as philosophy, religion, history, geography, language, studies of flora and fauna, and technology, interested him throughout his life. After reading the *Confucius Sinarum Philosophus*, Leibniz began to consider himself a follower of

Confucianism. He greatly admired ancient China's legendary model monarchs of Yao and Shun, Confucius and Mencius. He was particularly impressed with the Emperor Kangxi. It is interesting to note that more than three hundred years ago Leibniz warned

It would be highly foolish and presumptuous on our part, having newly arrived compared with them [the Chinese]…to want to condemn such an ancient doctrine [Confucianism] simply because it does not appear to agree at first glance with our ordinary scholastic notions.[5]

François Quesnay was another Western giant who admired Confucius. He was born in 1694, the son of a small landowner. In the early 17th century of the Enlightenment, China was perceived as a model of society, subject to the rule of law and the maximization of the happiness of the people. A large number of philosophers as well as statesmen and men of letters used Confucius and his ideas to further their arguments. Both in France and in England the fact that China, under the impulsion of Confucianism, had long since virtually abolished hereditary aristocracy, was used as a weapon to attack against hereditary privilege. Voltaire wrote: "The constitution of their [Chinese] empire is in truth the best that there is in the world… Four thousand years ago, when we did not know how to read, they knew everything essentially useful of which we boast today."[6]

Quesnay admired the rational principle of the Chinese constitution. In particular, he greatly admired the education system in China which helped the state select talented people for public service through a rigorous program of study and a competitive examination system. The Chinese idea about government through merit and learning rather than through heredity was greatly attractive to him. Quesnay considered China as a model while building its national economy on the basis of agriculture adhering to the reasons and principles regulated by "Heaven". In fact in his lifetime Quesnay was called "the Confucius of Europe."[7]

Criticisms against East Asian's Confucianism in "the Western standard" were not initiated by Fukuzawa. When he began to learn from the West, Western intellectuals changed their attitudes to China and even did not think that Chinese were even able to think properly, not to say to admire Chinese culture. "There reigns in Asia a servile spirit…," Montesquieu said, "It is impossible to find, in all the histories of this country, a single passage which discovers a free soul: we shall never see any thing there but the heroism of slavery."[8] In his influential study of formation of human character under various natural, social and economic conditions, Montesquieu concluded that the Chinese racial spirit was greedy, dishonest, industrious, and respectful of their elders.[9] In 1822, Hegel (1770-1831) depicted the Chinese character as follows: "In China, however, the distinction between Slavery and freedom is necessarily, not great, since all are equal before the Emperor – that is, all are alike degraded. As no honor exits, and no one has an individual right in respect of others, the consciousness of debasement predominates, and this easily passes into that of utter abandonment. With this abandonment is connected the great immorality of the Chinese. They are notorious for deceiving wherever they can. Friend deceives friend, and no one resents the attempt at deception on the part of another, if the deceit has not succeeded in its object, or comes to the knowledge of the person sought to be defrauded. Their frauds are most astutely and craftily performed, so that Europeans have to be painfully cautious in dealing with them."[10] In his essay *Of the Rise and Progress of the Arts and Sciences* published more than 200 years ago, the British philosopher and historian, David Hume observed: "In CHINA, there seems to be a pretty considerable stock of politeness and science, which, in the course of so many centuries, might naturally be expected to ripen into something more perfect and finished, than what has yet arisen from them. But CHINA is one vast empire, speaking one language, governed by one law, and sympathizing in the same manners. The authority of any teacher…was propagated easily from one corner of the empire to the other. None had courage to resist the torrent of popular opinion. And posterity was not bold enough to dispute what had been universally received by their ancestors. This seems to be one natural reason, why the sciences have made so slow a progress in that mighty empire." [11]

"Three hundred years ago," Tocqueville observed, "when the first Europeans came to China, they found that almost all the arts had reached a certain degree of improvement, and they were surprised that, having come so far, they had not gone further. Later on they found traces of profound knowledge that had been forgotten. The nation was a hive of industry; the greater part of its scientific methods was still in use, but science itself was dead. That made them to understand the strange immobility of mind found among this people. The Chinese, following their fathers' steps, had forgotten the reasons which guided them. They still used the formula without asking why....So the Chinese were unable to change anything. They had to drop the idea of improvement. They had to copy their ancestors the whole time in everything for fear of straying into impenetrable darkness if they deviated for a moment from their tracks. Human knowledge had almost dried up at the fount, and though the stream still flowed, it could neither increase nor change its course." [12]

When Fukuzawa started Western learning, "European intellectual fashion" had long ago changing from learning from and respecting Chinese civilization to that of neglecting and despising. In *On Liberty* of 1859, Mill compared the falling of China and the rise of Europe as follows

We have a warning example in China—a nation of much talent, and in some respects, even wisdom, owing to the rare good fortune of having been provided at an early period with a particularly good set of customs, the work, in some measure, of men to whom even the most enlightened European must accord, under certain limitations, the title of sages and philosophers....On the contrary, they have become stationary... They have succeeded beyond all hope in what English philanthropists are so industriously working at—in making a people all alike, all governing their thoughts and conduct by the same maxims and rules; and these are the fruits.

What has made the European family of nations an improving, instead of a stationary portion of mankind? Not any superior excellence in them, which, when it exists, exists as the effect not as the cause; but their remarkable diversity of character and culture.... Europe is, in my judgment, wholly indebted to this plurality of paths for its progressive and many-sided development.

Before he criticized the Chinese learning, Confucian practice in China had been criticized from multiple perspectives in the West. Montesquieu once said: "In deposit states each house is a separate government. As education therefore consists chiefly in social converse, it must be here very limited; all it does is to strike the heart with fear, and to imprint the understanding of a very simple notion of a few principles....Here therefore education is in some measure needless; to give something one must take away everything; and begin with making a bad subject in order to make a good slave."[13]

From these well-known criticisms about China and China's relative positions in the Western intellectual world when he was visiting the West, it would not be surprising to find that Fukuzawa believed that Confucian education, irrespective of its positive aspects, was inferior to the Western education with regard to creation of wealth, armament and general well-being. The long historical process through the Edo period generated a distinctively Japanese style of life and thought, which was destined to have an important influence on his thought. The society of the Edo period was characterized of the traditional stratification of classes into *samurai*, farmers, artisans, and merchants with an especially strict distinction made between the *samurai* and the remaining strata. In the area of education, distinctive schools were developed for each strata—the fief schools (*hanko* or *hangaku*) for the *samurai* and the *terakoya* for the commoners.

The *samurai* families of the Edo period not only used education to stabilize their own position but also came to further the cause of learning, especially through the systematized teaching of literary studies. Initially, the fief lords (*daimyo*), in order to further their own personal cultivation and, in turn, to maintain control of their fief governments, summoned Confucian scholars and military specialists (*heigakusha*) to conduct lectures which their chief vassals were required to attend. Learning during this period, being based upon *Shogunal* policy, was thoroughly imbued with Confucian thought. *Samurai* families originally availed themselves of the services of priests in Buddhist temples for their education. But by the Edo period, this class began to employ Confucian scholars to act as preceptors in fief schools they founded in the castle towns. During the early days of the Edo period, only a few fiefs had established fief schools but from about the middle of this period onward the spread of such institutions increased rapidly, culminating in a total of some 270 schools at the end of the period. The fief schools provided a comprehensive education for the *samurai* class. Instruction was centered about Chinese classics. This meant studies in Confucian doctrines and the history and literature of China. Elementary classes used the *Primer of Chinese Characters* (*Senjimon*) for practicing calligraphy and the *Brief History of Japan* (*Sanjikyo*) for practice in reading. Various other schools of Confucian thought developed during the early Edo period. However in 1790 the teaching of other schools of Confucianism was banned, and Chu Hsi was officially accepted as the orthodoxy. The curriculum was gradually expanded—in addition to Chinese studies, national learning and other subjects were introduced. Toward the end of the Edo period Western learning and medicine were also offered. As Nishikawa[14] observed, most of Japanese intellectuals were concerned with teaching young people how to read, but not interested in encouraging them to think creatively.

At the time commoners were inculcated with those virtues appropriate to members of their class and were trained in those skills needed in everyday life as befitted their station. What was very important for commoners was the training through apprenticeships (for both sexes) as well as daily activity groups such as the youth activity groups (*wakamonogumi*). The commoners depended their formal education in reading and writing on the *terakoya*, which were regarded as having developed from the educational facilities founded at Buddhist temples. The *terakoya* concerned themselves with practical matters and elementary education important to the daily life of the common people. The bulk of instruction in the *terakoya* was in reading and writing. By the end of the Edo period *terakoya* offering abacus calculation along with reading and writing increased in number. The number of these schools began to increase from the middle of the Edo period and by the end of that period they were common in the large cities. Due to the many *terakoya*, after the Education System Order (*Gakusei*) was proclaimed in 1872, it was possible within a very brief period to open elementary schools throughout the country.

Although the fief schools for the *samurai* and the *terakoya* for the commoners were representative educational institutions of the Edo period, other types of schools did exist. Another type of school which existed independently from the fief schools and the *terakoya* was the private school (*shijuku*), which developed from the "secret schools" of ancient and medieval times where a particularly close relationship existed between the teacher and the student and the object of instruction consisted in the transmission of confidential material relating to particular sects. By the end of the Edo period, various types of private institutions had developed specializing in such subjects as Chinese studies, calligraphy, abacus, National Learning (*kokugaku*), Western learning, and the like. As Western civilization was introduced to Japan, other types of private schools were organized for Western learning known as *Yogakujuku*. The private schools provided common educational facilities for both the *samurai* and the commoners. Fukuzawa's *Keio Gijuku* and other private schools at the time were to a great extent oriented toward Western learning and played an important role in the popular movement to realize "civilization and enlightenment". By the middle nineteenth century, the focus of Western learning had also shifted from medical science to technology and information having to do with national defense such as navigation, surveying, shipbuilding, and gunnery. The Tokugawa government developed many centers of Western learning; but by the close of the Edo period and during the early Restoration days many fiefs took it upon themselves to develop their own facilities for training in Western learning. Many private schools for Western learning were also developed in the Edo period. The most important private schools of Dutch Medicine were the Shosendo of Ito Genboku at Edo and the Tekijuku of Ogata Koan (1810-1863) at Osaka.

We mentioned that he specially identified two main problems in Confucianism—the lacking of mathematics in the realm of tangible and the lacking of the spirit of independence in the realm of intangible. He was largely alone among Western learning scholars in publicly condemning China and Chinese learning in the 1870s. He strongly opposed Chinese learning in his popular works of the mid-1870s. He considered Chinese learning irrelevant to the new civilization of commerce and equality. Chinese learning was condemned for being impractical and conservative. He argued that Chinese learning emphasized nothing but the past. It was a great obstacle to progress because it promoted (immobile) hierarchy. It encouraged a value system which perversely sustained self-deceit, insincerity, flattery, slavishness to others, and greed. There was nothing so vividly portraying the consequence of Chinese learning as China's submission to the hands of foreigners.

## Confucian Gentleman and His Spirit of Independence and Learning

Having not and yet affecting to have, empty and yet affecting to be full, straitened and yet affecting to be at ease—it is difficult with such characteristics to have constancy.
Confucius (7:26)

Confucian tradition believes in the existence of laws governing human life as well as nature. *The Great Learning* propounds the existence of law in everything: "If we wish to carry our knowledge to the utmost, we must investigate the principles of all things we come into contact with, for the intelligent mind of man is certainly formed to know, and there is not a single thing in which its principles do not inhere. But as long as all principles are not investigated, man's knowledge is incomplete." This belief in the existence of rational laws may be what enabled Confucian civilization to accept with confidence (once social stability was guaranteed) modern mathematics, modern science and technology, and Western rational thought. Sciences have been universally accepted as "trustworthy explanations" of natural phenomena in the Confucian regions.

There is no fixed concrete faith in Confucianism; but Confucius (7: 17) advocated lifelong learning: "Learn as if you could not reach your object, and were always fearing also you should lose it." According to Confucius, "The object of the superior man is truth. Food is not his object. There is ploughing—even in that there is sometimes want. So with learning; emolument may be found in it. The superior man is anxious lest he should not get truth; he is not anxious lest poverty should come upon him." Confucius (15: 39) promoted education for everyone: "There being instruction, there will be no distinction of classes."(Equal opportunity in education and determining social status by effort and by learning are the bases by which equality may be realized among men.) In the ancient Confucianism a gentleman learns for self-cultivating rather than serving some fixed "symbol" or goal, like the emperor or nation. Fukuzawa "Westernized" (or "modernized") the image of the Confucian gentleman according to the time.

For Fukuzawa, learning is the key to independence. Independence was the purpose and learning was the means for attaining and preserving it. He recognized that China valued the teachings of Confucius and Mencius and the Confucianism of Japan studied the same doctrines, the results of knowledge diffusion were different in the two countries. He held that Confucianism in China had no competition and it became intoxicated with itself. Nevertheless, in Japan

Confucianism was not so corrupt as in China as it was faced with competition. As the Confucian scholars were mostly *samurai*, they were naturally retained health and had active interests in literary and artistic pursuits. He thus did not lose the hope for Japan because Japan had more spirit of independence than China. He held: "With that spirit, they guided their pupils toward a vigorous life style, and all the people in the country above the samurai class were naturally influenced in this way. Therefore, one may see that the whole society of Japan was ready for new development and reform."[15]

In comparison to the West, he found many shortcomings of Japan. In *Gakumon no Susume*, he described that the Confucian students spent many years making voluminous copies of Confucian books, but finally they would find no use for industrious learning and became ignorant and penniless.[16] In *Bunmeiron no Gairyaku*, he compared learning between the West and Japan.[17] He observed that learning arose in the West among common people, whereas learning was initiated by the government in Japan. In the West learning was the business of scholars, whereas in Japan learning was the business of government. He was greatly impressed by the tradition of academic independence he encountered in the West. He argued that universities should not be subservient to the ideology of the state. In *The Independence of Learning* in 1883, he asked for independence of learning from politics. He pointed out that learning and politics share the same ideals in promoting the fortunes of a nation, but they are different. Scholars are not politicians, and vice versa. The interest of scholars is far removed from the realities of the present society, while that of politicians is mainly concerned with every matter of the people. Learning immensely influences society. This does not mean that the scholars would be efficient administrators. He argued that when politics and learning are separate and independent, one field must not interfere with the other, but that professionals must concentrate on their respective work, never meddling in the affairs of the other. He suggested that for the benefit of society as a whole, education and politics should be strictly separated. A strict prohibition of their intermingling will be an advantage to society and increase happiness of the specialists. In Japan, for the separation to be effective, he asked for independence of learning from politics. In particular, he wanted the schools under the direct control of the Ministry of Education and the Ministry of Industry to be independent of those institutions.

He held that genuine learning should be achieved with studies and discussions from a free point of view, without taking account of political situations. For education to be independent of politics, he considered that schools should be run by principals and teachers who are totally unrelated to the government. They should also have no prejudice in politics. As long as those in charge are free of politics both in mind and in position, studying or discussing any subject would have no harm to students and society. He proposed to separate all the public schools in the country from the Ministry of Education, placing them under the supervision of the Imperial Household, which will grant control of each school to a private citizen of organized ability and provide financial aid from the Imperial Household treasury.

## The Ancient Confucian and His Attitudes Towards Learning

Fukuzawa held that education should provide practical knowledge and rational thinking and students should endeavor for independence for himself and his family. If individuals are independent, the nation would naturally become independent. In order to examine relations between Fukuzawa's attitudes towards learning and education and the essence of the ancient Confucianism, we now examine learning and the role of scholar in Confucianism.[18] It should be noted that in Confucianism "knowledge" is mainly referred to the knowledge of man and society. Although Confucianism provided some visionary views about nature, it was little concerned with natural sciences.

Confucius was living in an age where multiple states and cultures were competing and there was no "global" order. Partly due to technological changes, some states were disappearing because of the competition. Under such circumstances, learning was obviously a key factor in building national strength and national survival. When Confucius (13: 9) went to Wei, he observed, "How numerous are the people!" His disciple asked him what more should be done for the people. Confucius said: "Enrich them." And what then? "Teach them." Confucius (13: 29-30) emphasized discipline: "Let a good man teach the people seven years, and they may then likewise employed in war....To lead an uninstructed people to war is to throw them away." According to Confucius (4: 8), different subjects of learning play varied roles in the mind: "It is by the Odes that the mind is aroused. It is by the Rules of Propriety that the character is established. It is from Music that the perfection is received." According to Confucius (13: 5), both learning and thinking are significant, for knowledge accumulation and problem solving; and a man must be able to apply what he has learned: "Learning without thought is labor lost; thought without learning is perilous," and "Though a man may be able to recite the three hundred Odes, yet if, when entrusted with a governmental charge, he knows not how to act, or if, when sent to any quarter on a mission, he cannot give his replies unassisted, notwithstanding the extent of his learning, of what practical use is it?"

In Confucianism, to become human is to behave morally and to learn constantly. Birth, race, and wealth were not considered the key measures of human quality. Confucius, Mencius and Hsün Tzu were born into humble conditions; they had to learn many things just to survive. This may explain the Confucian attitudes towards human life and society. Social environment has a great impact, if it is not absolutely determining, on a man's thought. In a deep sense, the ancient Greek culture had less democratic elements than the ancient Confucianism, even though the former proposed a conception of democracy (distorted as it was, in today's understanding).

In Confucianism, to be socially superior means to serve society in the superior way. Confucius (16: 9) classified men according to knowledge: "Those who are born with the possession of knowledge are the highest class of men. Those who learn, and so readily get possession of knowledge, are the next. Those who learn after they meet with difficulties are another class next to these. As to those who meet with difficulties and yet do not learn—they are the lowest of the people." And he explicitly stated that he never met anyone born with the possession of knowledge. For Confucius, nothing is so important in distinguishing men as learning through education, working, communication, or playing, because he claimed (17: 2) that "By nature, men are nearly alike; by practice, they get to be far apart." One should seek the truth and endure the consequences. "If a man in the morning hear the right way," Confucius (2: 15) averred, "he may die in the evening without regret." "If the scholar be not grave," Confucius (1: 8) argued, "he will not call forth any veneration and his learning will not be solid. Hold faithfulness and sincerity as first principles. Have no friends not equal to yourself. When you have faults, do not fear to abandon them." Since he held that it is mainly learning that makes men different, it is reasonable (15: 30) to constantly emphasize learning and improving: "To have faults and not to reform—this, indeed, should be pronounced having faults."

With regard to the relationship among learning, benevolence, knowledge, sincerity, straightforwardness, boldness, and firmness, Confucius (17: 8) revealed: "There is the love of being benevolent without the love of learning—the beclouding here leads to a foolish simplicity. There is the love of knowing without the love of learning—the beclouding here leads to dissipation of mind. There is the love of being sincere without the love of learning—the beclouding here leads to an injurious disregard of consequences. There is the love of straightforwardness without the love of learning—the beclouding here leads to rudeness. There is the love of boldness without love of learning—the beclouding here leads to insubordination. There is the love of firmness without the loving of learning—the beclouding here leads to extravagant conduct." To effectively employ knowledge, Mencius (8: 8) suggested: "Those who keep the Mean, train up those who do not, and those who have abilities, train up those who have not, and hence men rejoice in having fathers and elder brothers who are possessed of virtue and talent. If they who keep the Mean spurn those who do not, and they who have abilities spurn those who have not, then the space between them—those so gifted and ungifted—will not admit an inch." According to *The Great Learning*: "It is only the truly virtuous man who can love or who can hate others. To see men of worth and not able to raise them to office; to raise them to office, but not so quickly;—this is disrespect. To see bad men and not be able to remove them; to remove them, but not to do so to a distance:—this is weakness. To love those whom men hate, and to those whom men love:—this is to outrage the natural feeling of men. Calamities cannot fail to come down on him who does so.' Thus, we see that the sovereign has a great course to pursue. He must show entire self-devotion and sincerity to attain it, and by pride and extravagance he will fail of it."

Hsün Tzu (1: 1) said that learning should be conducted through self-examination: "Learning must never be concluded.... In broadening his learning, the gentleman each day examines himself so that his awareness will be discerning and his actions without excess." He recommended (1: 8) that "Learning continues until death and only then does it stop. Thus, though the methods employed to learn come to a conclusion, the purpose of learning must never, even for an instant, be put aside. Those who undertake learning become men; those who neglect it become as wild beasts." Hsün Tzu also (1: 10) distinguished the attitudes towards learning between the gentleman and the small man: "In antiquity men undertook learning for the sake of self-improvement; today people undertake learning for the sake of others. The learning of the gentleman is used to refine his character. The learning of the petty man is used like ceremonial offerings of birds and calves." "When a man's knowledge is sufficient to attain," Confucius (15: 33) portrayed, "and his virtue is not sufficient to enable him to hold, whatever he may have gained, he will lose again. When his knowledge is sufficient to attain, and he has virtue enough to hold fast, if he cannot govern with dignity, the people will not respect him. When his knowledge is sufficient to attain, and he has virtue enough to hold fast; when he governs also with dignity, yet if he try to move the people contrary to the rules of propriety—full excellence is not reached." Confucius was neither an optimist nor pessimist. He had a good grasp of man's limitation as a social being: "Alas! How is the path of the Mean untrodden!"

## The Confucian Utilitarianism in Learning and His Practical Learning

"Confucianism is more rationalist and sober," Max Weber observed, "in the sense of the absence and the rejection of all non-utilitarian yardsticks, than any other ethical system, with the possible exception of J. Bentham's."[19] The ancient Confucianism was constructed by the three thinkers who had to earn their own living by educating pupils and serving three states. In fact, Confucius established the first private school in China. He did not advocate teaching without pay; but Confucius (7: 7) did say, "From the man bringing his bundle of dried flesh for my teaching upwards, I have never refused instruction." Since knowledge is useful in Confucian society and pupils will economically benefit from their education, teachers who conduct education independent of government should charge pupils. For Confucius (8: 12), self-interest is the basic motive for common people's behavior: "It is not easy to find a man who has learned for three years without thinking of becoming an official." To show honest and respect, students paid their education fees to Confucius, even though these fees were not fixed, changeable according to one family's social and economic conditions. It is reasonable expect that in the ancient Confucianism learning is for earning as well.

Fukuzawa distinguished between two categories of learning: "real" (or useful) learning (*jitsugaku*) and "false/empty" learning (*kyogako*). Real learning helped people to attain freedom and independence. The Western learning belonged to this category. False learning was the kind that taught knowledge and skills but molded people into disciplined subjects or vassals, useful to the state or lord. He argued: "Someone who has penetrated the mysteries of the Confucian Classics and Books of History but cannot conduct a simple business transaction I would say he knew little of the 'learning' of commerce." This attitude is Confucian as well.

He held that the Japanese neo-Confucian learning belonged to the category of empty learning. He argued that writing, bookkeeping, the abacus, geography, philosophy, economics, ethics, these are all ordinary human useful learning (*jitsugaku*), which should be studied by everyone, high and low. Through learning, men would be able to do their best in their respective "callings". Learning would also enable their families to obtain independence and the state could enjoy independence too. He was against ignorant people because they were unenlightened. He firmly believed that civilization would arise not from the government, not from the lower people, but from the middle class such as men like Adam Smith and James Watt. The new middle class in Japan should be created under the leadership of enlightened from *samurai*, and recruited from the merchants and artisans who would learn *jitsugaku*. The most important influence from the West, which he most clearly exemplified and fostered was British utilitarianism and liberalism. Linked closely to this was the prevailing belief in human progress through the wider application of the methods of the natural sciences. Nevertheless, toward the end of his life, he expressed the conviction that moral and religious regeneration of the Japanese was indispensable to their future progress.

In the 1868 inauguration speech of his school, he stated: "What places Western learning apart from all other learnings is that it is a true product of nature and it rides with reason; it teaches the ways of humankind and it moderates between an individual and society."[20] For him, the spirit of the new *jitsugaku* was characterized of doubt and experiment. The laws of nature could only be discovered through taking nothing for granted and constant experiment, the laws of nature. He observed that when the Western science was making progresses, the scholars of the Orient were concerned themselves with the Chinese classics and put no attention to useful learning and practice. He pointed out that with regard to the matter of physical laws the Japanese Confucian scholars knew no more than an ignorant housemaid. He also held that East Asia could not make progress because they did not have systematical knowledge. As there was no systematical knowledge, progresses in some fields might have been accomplished merely due to blind chance.

He held that it is due to lack of interest in the laws of nature that Japan failed to progress. Japan was mainly concerned with particular kind of knowledge, ethnical knowledge, but had little interest in ethically neutral scientific knowledge. He accepted that it is wrong to believe that virtue is the sole element of civilization. What had caused progress in civilization was not virtue but scientific knowledge. There had been little progress in virtue since ancient times. Moralists and saints had done almost nothing but comments on the principles laid down by Christ and Confucius. They did not turn the Ten Commandments into eleven or the Five Relations into six. But in scientific knowledge, "we know", he claims, "a hundred things where the ancients knew one. We despise what they feared, mock what they marveled at."[21]

With regard to knowledge, creation, and accumulation, he emphasized observation and conceptual and theoretical construction. Without observation, theory leads to nowhere; without theory, observation is only observation. In the 1880s, he often referred to regular order (*seisoku*) in education. By this he meant a correct order in which subjects should be introduced to students so that they would understand and assimilate the nature of modern civilization. According to him, this order should start with mathematics and physics, as the two fields were the basis to all modern knowledge and thinking. Then, students should be introduced to chemistry, geography, social studies, ethics, literature, and other subjects. Scientific training was necessary for everyone in modern society and even those who wanted to become artists should receive scientific training first.

## "Learn and Earn, Earn and Learn"

As mentioned before, the three ancient Confucian sages, Confucius, Mencius, and Hsün Tze, did not neglect the importance of earning from learning. In fact, they all lived on incomes from teaching and serving governments. He was born into poverty and his living was dependent on his writings. His father was a scholar; but had to live a miserable life in the feudal system where true learning was not useful for earning living. When he was young, if one was not born into good fortune environment, pursuing high learning could not be used to earn a living. In particular, Japan was very poor and common people could not have the luxury of getting education from the public funds. It is reasonable to expect that he taught his students to have a proper sense of money. He encouraged his students to do business. His students formed the first generation of Japan's business elite.

"Learning and earn, earn and learn" is his motto in his approach to modern education.[22] In 1898, he advised: "Seeking employment is a kind of hardship....In times of war, become a career soldier. When poetry is in vogue, take up the study of poetry."[23] He told his nephew Nakamigawa: "Learn and earn, earn and learn, then you can obtain both the status of a scholar and of a rich man, and for the first time you can change the mind of the people of Japan." In his *Speech What I Ask for the Worlds of Commerce and Industry* in 1884, he related: "I am no less concerned about the prosperity of business and industry than are the businessmen and industrialists....Business and industry are like a mother to scholarship."[24] As a modern scholar, he recognized that in a national level, economic conditions go before scholarship.

He believed that to build Japan into a wealthy country the country should cultivate entrepreneurial skill. Efforts of entrepreneurial individuals would enrich the country and they would also become wealthy. He entered into the business world when he found that he could realize greater royalties from his writings if he published his books. Maruzen was established along the lines of a joint stock company, the first in Japan. The first Maruzen was opened in Yokohama, selling Western books, stationery, clothing and pharmaceuticals. Soon after the beginning of the 1870s, branches in Tokyo, Osaka, Kyoto, and Nagoya were opened. Although he did not directly operate the business, he was supposed to be the primary force behind its business plan, a major investor, and a business consultant,[25] He was considered effectively the strongest man in the management of the company. As Hopper observed, "He was helped in his own efforts to obtain wealth by the fact that he knew the primary government players in Japan's development…. He also counted many of the new industrial leaders among his friends and associates."[26]

In *Gakumon no Susume*, Fukuzawa taught that without practical application, learning is equivalent to ignorance. He esteemed knowledge; but for him learning is an art of human life, rather than life itself. In *Gakumon no Susume*, he pointed out: "Until now there have been very few Chinese scholars who were good at running their households, and very few clever merchants who were also good at poetry."[27] For him, what are useless include "knowing strange words or reading ancient and difficult literature or enjoying poetry and writing verse and other such accomplishments which are of no practical use in the world."[28]

According to Fukuzawa, *Jitsugaku* should not be confined to a few scholars; all people should be engaged in pursuing it. To spread it, primary education should emphasize *Jitsugaku*. People should know the laws of nature. When they build houses, they should take note of the mechanical laws involved in building. If they don't know the physical laws, they are not better even than horses who eat their food without wondering what it is made of. Nevertheless, he held that higher education, or university education, was appropriate for a few gifted individuals who were willing to work for the independence of the country. He did not think that education was something to be given equally to all. In particular, he did not encourage education for the illiterate poor. He did not ask for spreading education to women as he believed that women could not benefit from education. He held that the *samurai* and wealthier merchants and farmers could all benefit from full education. But the peasant class was a potentially dangerous force. As in Europe, if they received an education, peasants might rise in rebellion against the establishment. That in turn would weaken the state, giving the Western nations a perfect opportunity to step in and take control of Japan. For him, general education was promoted for the independence of individual and higher education for that of the nation. In the first decade of Meiji, there was no institution of higher learning in Japan.[29] In the country, there were few qualified students and professors were employed from abroad. As far as modern learning is concerned, the educational level of most Japanese was not higher than the elementary level. Even adult students at his school could only read elementary textbooks published in the United States and England. Only by 1877, there were a sufficient number of students for Japan to start a university. Tokyo Daiguko (later named the Imperial University of Tokyo) was established then. In the beginning, practically all the professors in this institution were foreigners. Only by 1890 he organized the university departments as a division of Keio Gijuku.

## The Rationality in the Ancient Confucianism and His Role of Scholar

"A non-bounded great mind either eschews society, taking refuge deep in the mountains like Lao Tze, or struggles in human society, even in a mad fashion, like Nietzsche. A mind that knows neither genuine freedom nor duty cannot even distinguish between proper reciprocity and sheer begging."[30] As shown before, Fukuzawa's social order is built neither on the law nor on duty (benevolence), but a kind of combination of the law and duty. We now examine the ancient Confucian attitudes toward these issues.

In her Address to the General Assembly of the Church of Scotland in 1988, the Prime Minister of Great Britain, Margaret Thatcher, addressed: "We Parliamentarians can legislate for the rule of law. You the Church can teach the life of faith." Rational Confucianism—a doctrine that never asks for faith or a belief in personalized God— repeatedly emphasizes duty (rather than blind obedience) for men to become human; the American civilization, which is free, relies on religion. Confucianism is not religion. Nevertheless, there is no sign in the ancient Confucianism that religion is intolerable. Leibniz observed in 1716: "Initially, one may doubt if the Chinese do recognize, or have recognized, spiritual substances. But upon reflection, I believe that they did, although perhaps they did not recognize these substances as separated, and existing quite apart from matter".[31] Confucius (2: 24), who rarely commented on matters of spirit, did say: "For a man to sacrifice to a spirit which does not belong to him is flattery. To see what is right and not to do it is want of courage." And when a disciple asked Confucius about serving the spirits of the dead, he replied (11: 12): "while you are not able to serve men, how you can serve their spirits?" When the disciple inquired about death, Confucius answered: "While you do not know life, how can you know about death?"

Although Confucianism does not propose any personalized God, this does not mean that it does not believe in the existence of natural law or creation. "The course of Nature is constant" claimed Hsün Tzu (17: 1): "it does not survive because of the actions of a Yao; it does not perish because of the actions of a Jie. If you respond to the constancy of Nature's course with good government, there will be good fortune; if you respond to it with disorder, there will be misfortune." "How can glorifying Heaven and contemplating it, be as good as tending its creatures and regulating them?" Hsün Tzu (17: 14) asked. "How can obeying Heaven and singing it hymns of praise be better than regulating what Heaven has mandated and using it? How can anxiously watching for the season and waiting what it brings, be as good as responding to the season and exploiting it? How can depending on things to increase naturally be better than developing their natural capacities so as to transform them? How can contemplating things and expecting them to serve you be as good as administering them so that you do not miss the opportunities that are present? How can brooding over for the origins of things be better than assisting what perfects them? Accordingly, if you can cast aside the concerns proper to Man in order to speculate about what belongs to Heaven, you will miss the essential nature of the myriad things." Mencius (4: 1) averred, "Opportunities of time vouchsafed by Heaven are not equal to advantages of situation afforded by the Earth, and advantages of situation afforded by the Earth are not equal to the union arising from the accord of Men." Mencius (7: 8) reveals, "A man must first despise himself, and then others will despise him. A family must destroy itself, and then others will destroy it. A kingdom must first smite itself, and then others will smite it. This is illustrated in the passage of the Tai Jia: 'When Heaven sends down calamities, it is still possible to escape them. When we occasion the calamities ourselves, it is not possible any longer to live."

Confucianism does not promote faith in a personalized God; and there is no group identity such as racism or nationalism in the ancient Confucianism. The lack of a "local identity" was perhaps a consequence of Confucius' experience of traveling to varied cultures and being employed by different governments, and his rational attitude toward human life. During his lifetime, he observed how different cultures interacted with each other under competitive conditions.

By the way, it is worth noting that the Chinese had built more than one powerful empire before the heralds of the West sailed into East Asia. Nevertheless, these Chinese empires—except the foreign ones under the Mongols and Manchus—had not adopted extreme expansionist strategies. One may find two factors—economic and ideological—to explain the lack of imperialism. The first has to do with China's economic geography. Given the traditional transportation technology and traditional weapons, the empires would not have found economic benefit in expanding beyond a certain size. The second factor is that, when China became strong, Confucianism was the national ideology. Since it does not claim any superiority in spirit or truth and signifies harmonious co-existence of different peoples,

Confucianism can hardly be employed to encourage imperialism. The Confucian attitude towards other cultures is best illustrated by the Master's own saying: "When I walk along with other two others, they may serve me as my teachers. I will select their good qualities and follow them, their bad qualities and avoid them." Mencius believed: "The respectful do not despise others. The economical do not plunder others."

The "core identity" of Confucianism is the Way, that is, the truth. No personalized or socialized symbol plays the role of arbitrator of the truth in Confucianism. Confucius (4: 16) said, "my doctrine is that of an all-pervading unity."…the other disciples asked, "What do his words mean?" The disciple Zeng answered, "The doctrine of our master is to be true to the principles of our nature and the benevolent exercise of them to others—this and nothing more." Confucius (2: 14) asserted: "The superior man is catholic and not partisan. The mean man is a partisan and not catholic."

He did not believe in any religion. He did not advocate for spread of any religion for saving Japan from foreign threats. He emphasized education and the role of scholar for modernizing Japan. Like in the ancient Confucians, he wanted the scholar to "be true to the principles of our nature and the benevolent exercise of them to others". He held that the scholar provided society the virtue example by being independent of the government, rather than by serving it. He believed that the first duty of scholars in Japan was to awaken the people to a sense of independence. He said: "When there are no qualified men among the teachers, no matter how much the school curriculum is improved or whatever textbooks are published, no great results can be expected."[32] A scholar was not only to do research and accumulate knowledge. It was of greater importance to awaken the power of reasoning or the sense of independence of the people. If the scholar did not bear this duty thoroughly, Japan's independence in this competitive world would not be realized. Neither government officials, nor farmers and merchants, nor scholars of classical Chinese and Japanese, could demonstrate a truly independent way of life for people to emulate. The task for civilizing Japan had to rely on the scholars of Western studies. Nevertheless, he observed that many scholars of Western learning were lured into government posts.

He held that the spirit of independence in Japan was weak. It was not sufficient for the nation to establish schools, industry, and military forces for Japan to become a civilized nation. Japan needed the spirit of independence. He said, "In ancient time government weakened power of people; in present government weakens spirit of people."[24] He warned that as the state expanded its power, the spirit of independence of the people, which was the basis of national independence, might decline. To prevent this negative relationship between the state power and the people's spirit of independence, scholars should be independent of the government and show the people the correct ways for civilization. He suggested that to progress more rapidly, it was important to change minds and spirits of the people. Moreover, he did not think the government, merchants, farmers, nativist scholars, and Chinese learning scholars suitable for the task. He also denied the Western learning scholars reliable for the task because they were busy offering their skills to the government. He challenged Western learning scholars to become reformers and examples to the people. He held that scholars could complete the task by keeping themselves out of government service and assuming a private position from which to pursue learning, law, and commerce. Acting as private persons and pursuing personal goals, scholars would serve the people and the nation and cumulatively contribute to the advance of civilization. He also believed that since scholars were also part of the people, their personal goals would conflict with the interests of the people.

# 5

# Competition and Economic Development

If the search for riches is sure to be successful, though I should
become a gatekeeper with whip in hand to get them, I will do so. As the
search may not be successful, I will follow after that which I love.
Confucius (7: 12)

With the demand for opening up, Commodore Matthew Perry
steamed into Tokyo Bay with his "black ships of evil mien" more than
150 years ago. Before the black ships arrived on July 8, 1853, the
Tokugawa shoguns had run Japan for 250 years as a reclusive feudal
state. Carrying a letter from America's president, Millard Fillmore, and
punctuating his message with cannon fire, Commodore Perry ordered
Japan's rulers to drop their barriers and open the country to trade. In
1868, a group of *samurai* from the domains of *Satsuma* and *Choshu*
overthrew *Tokugawa* shogun and proclaimed the restoration of the
Emperor Meiji as the head of state. After 1868, the former *samurai*
became key economic policy makers in the *Meiji* government. These
officials destroyed much of the *Tokugawa* feudal system and
developed Japanese capitalist institutions within 20 years.[1] The new
institutions facilitated Japan's industrial revolution. In the one and a
half centuries, Japan emerged as one of history's great economic

successful stories. When America's black ships forced open Japan, nobody could have predicted that the resource-poor "tiny island" would become the world's second economic power. Japan had mastered the art of opening up on its own terms. Before and after those black ships steamed into Tokyo Bay, some other countries were also opened to trade by western cannon. What set Japan apart was its ability to decide for itself how to make the process of opening up to "enrich the country and strengthen the army." The per capita GNP of Japan from the end of the nineteenth century to the beginning of the twentieth century is estimated to have been one tenth of that of the United States, one sixth of that of England, and one quarter or one fifth of that of the Netherlands, Germany, and France. Nevertheless, Japan carried out industrialization rapidly. Japan had become equal to or slightly less developed than that of European countries in the first quarter of the twentieth century.

Sagers addresses an important question related to Japan's modernization: "Facing potential Western colonization, the desire for wealth and power was certainly understandable, but what was it that philosophically prepared early Meiji Japanese government leaders to accept capitalist institutions of economic organization?"[2] Sagers also observed: "Although historians have understood the importance of the Meiji period to the later evolution of the developmental state, there has been surprisingly little analysis and discussion of the role of economic thought in the government's industrial policy."[3] Sagers listed several reasons for the negligence. First, the problem is essentially multi-disciplinary. Nevertheless, economic historians had been mainly concerned with the role of economic aggregates such as capital accumulation, labor supply and technology transfer, but they tended to neglect the thought behind the policies. On the other hand, intellectual historians had tended to study the rise of Japanese political nationalism and national consciousness. Different from Sagers who is concerned with the formation of the economic ideas in the early years of Japan's Westernization, this chapter focuses on Fukuzawa's ideas about political economy and their relations to the ancient Confucianism.

Yagi argued: "By his theory of 'civilization', Fukuzawa provided the Japanese with the perspective that would conciliate the antagonism between liberalism and interventionism with a time span. It is interesting that this trait survived for a century in Japan and molded the economic policy in her post-1945 industrial state."[4] Nevertheless, an interesting question is how Fukuzawa could have been able to timely deny the Japanese traditions and become Westernized so rapidly. In *Gakumon no Susume*, he emphasized the role of education on economic conditions: "Only those who strive to be educated and are capable of reasoning will earn rank and riches while those without will become poor and lowly."[5] His essay *Discourse on Industry* provided the guidelines for the government to promote the industrial revolution and free trading. In the essay, he pointed out: "Forty years have passed since the visit of the American fleet,…the development of industry is the sole stagnant area…. To compete internationally in trade, the captains of industry need to have a *samurai* sense of Puritanism, for example, being upright, honest, and stable, and they should have the requisite scientific knowledge."[6]

## Minimum Government Intervention in the Ancient Confucianism and His Economic Liberty

There is no evil to which the mean man, dwelling retired, will not proceed, but when he sees a superior man, he instantly tries to distinguish himself, concealing his evil, and displaying what is good.
*The Great Learning*

Influenced by Adam Smith, Fukuzawa advocated for economic freedom with proper government intervention. Nevertheless, freedom in pursuing one's self interest was not foreign to the ancient Confucianism. Confucius is far more positive about social and moral implications of wealth than Adam Smith.[7] The relation between wealth and virtue held by Confucianism is described by *The Great Learning:* "Virtue is the root; wealth is the result. If he make the root his secondary object, and the result his primary, he will only wrangle with his people, and teach them rapine. Hence, the accumulation of wealth is the way to scatter the people; and the letting it be scattered among them is the way to collect the people." To properly govern a state, according to Confucius, "there must be reverent attention to business, and sincerity; economy in expenditure, and love for men; and the employment of the people at the proper time."

For society to effectively operate there should be division of labor. The division is based on the contribution. "The getting those various articles in exchange for grain," reasoned Mencius (5: 4), "is not oppressive to the potter and the founder, and the potter and the founder in their turn, in exchanging their various articles for grain, are not oppressive to the husbandman....Great men have their proper business, and little men have their proper business. Moreover, in the case of any single individual, whatever articles he can require are ready to his hand, being produced by the various handicraftsmen. If he must first make them for his own use, this way of doing would keep the whole empire running about upon the roads. Hence, there is the saying, 'Some labor with their minds, and some labor with their strength. Those who labor with their minds govern others; those who labor with their strength are governed by others. Those who are governed by others support them; those who govern others are supported by them.' This is a principle universally recognized."

In Confucian tradition, the economic welfare of the people is the indicator of the goodness of government. "It never has been that", Mencius (1: 7) claims, "the rulers of a state where such results were seen – the old wearing silk and eating flesh, and the black-haired people suffering neither from hunger nor cold – did not attain to the Imperial dignity." According to Mencius (1: 3), "The condition in which the people nourish their living and bury their dead without any feeling against any is the first step of Royal Government." Mencius (3: 5) held that a ruler attain the imperial dignity by practicing liberty policy: "If a ruler give honor to men of talents and virtue and employ the able, so that offices shall all be filled by individuals of distinction and mark, then all the scholars of the empire will be pleased, and wish to stand in his court. If, in the market place of his capital, he levy a ground rent on the shops but do not tax the goods, or enforce the proper regulations without levying a ground rent, then all the traders of the empire will be pleased, and wish to store their goods in his market place. If, at his frontier passers, there be an inspection of persons, but no taxes charged on goods or other articles, then all the travelers of the empire will be pleasured, and wish to make their tours on his roads. If he requires that the husbandmen give their mutual aid to cultivate the public field, and erect no other taxes from them – then all the husbandmen of the empire will be pleased, and wish to plough in his fields. If from the occupations of the shops in his market place, he do not exact the fine of the individual idler, or of the hamlet's quota of cloth, then all the people of the empire will be pleasured, and wish to come and be his people. If a ruler can truly practice these five things, then the people in the neighboring kingdoms will look up to him as a parent. From the first birth of mankind till now, never has any one led children to attack their parent. Thus such a ruler will not have an enemy in all the empire, and he who has no enemy in the empire is the minister of Heaven. Never has there been a ruler in such a case who did not attain to the Imperial dignity."

In Confucian tradition, it is held that a benevolent government minimizes its intervention in people's business. For Confucius, an ideal government is one that people are not aware of its existence. Confucius (8: 18) proclaims: "How majestic was the manner in which Shun and Yu held possession of the empire, as if it were nothing to them!" People should not be interfered in their pursuit of self-interest. "With a territory", Mencius (1: 5) describes, "which is only a hundred *li* square, it is possible to attain the Imperial dignity. If your Majesty will indeed dispense a benevolent government to the people – being sparing in the use of punishments and fines, and making the taxes and levies light, so causing that the fields shall be ploughed deep, and the weeding of them be carefully attended to, and that the strong-bodied, during their days of leisure, shall cultivate their filial piety, fraternal respectfulness, sincerity and trustfulness, serving thereby, at home, their fathers and elder brothers, and, abroad, their elders and superiors – you will then have a people who can be employed."

Hsün Tzu (10: 17) backs that taking less from people would benefit the government: "A policy of 'not benefiting the people yet taking benefits from them' provides fewer benefits than that of 'benefiting from the people only after first having benefited them.' A policy of 'using the people but not loving them' results in fewer achievements than that of 'using the people only after having demonstrated love for them.' A policy of 'benefiting the people and only then receiving benefits from them' produces fewer benefits than that of 'benefiting the people but receiving no benefits from them.' A policy of 'using the people only after having bestowed love on them' results in less benefit than that of 'loving the people but making no use of them.' One who 'provides benefits but does not take them' and who 'loves but does not use them' will capture the world. One who 'benefits the people and only then receives benefits from them' and who 'uses' the people only after having first bestowed love on them' will protect his altars of soil and grain. One who 'does not benefit the people yet takes benefits from them' and who 'uses them but does not love them' will imperil his nation." Hsün Tzu (9: 5) pointed out that heavy tax is to destroy country: "One who attends merely to collecting taxes is following a way that invites bandits, fattens his enemies, dooms his own country, and threatens his own survival. Accordingly, the intelligent lord does not treat this path." According to Hsün Tzu (10: 4), "If one taxes lightly the cultivated fields and outlying districts, imposes excises uniformly at the border stations and in the marketplace, keeps statistical records to reduce the number of merchants and traders, initiates only rarely projects requiring the labor of the people, and does not take the farmers from their fields except in the off-season, the state will be wealthy. This may be described as 'allowing the people a generous living through the exercise of government."

120

Mencius (13: 26) reprehends the extreme poles (socialism and capitalism): "The principle of the philosopher Yang was – 'Each one for himself.' Though he might have benefited the whole empire by plucking out a single hair, he would not have done it. The philosopher Mo loves all equally. If by rubbing smooth his whole body from the crown to the heel, he would have benefited the empire, he would have done it. Zimo holds a medium between these. By holding that medium, he is nearer the right. But by holding it without leaving room for the exigency of circumstances, it becomes like their holding their one point. The reason why I hate that holding to one point is the injury it does to the way of right principle. It takes up one point and disregards a hundred others." Hsün Tzu (10: 13) denounced equalitarianism: "If the methods of the Mohists are thoroughly carried out, then although the principle of frugality has been raised up, the world will have ever-increasing poverty; although combat has been condemned the world will daily be embroiled in strife; although the people toil away at bitter tasks, wearing themselves out and suffering from fatigue, they will increasingly be without accomplishment; although ruefully suffering and enduring hardship in condemning music each day, they will be less harmonious."

Confucianism does not advocate economic equality; nevertheless, it warns against likely negative consequences brought about by inequalities, especially by poverty. Mencius (8: 2) argued, "Let a governor conduct his rule on principles of equal justice....If a governor will try to please everybody, he will find the days not sufficient for his work." "They are only men of education," Mencius (1: 7) related, "who, without a certain livelihood are able to maintain a fixed heart. As to the people, if they have not a certain livelihood, it follows that they will not have a fixed heart. And if they have not a fixed heart, there is nothing, which they will not do, in the way of self-abandonment, of moral deflection, of depravity, and of wild license. When they thus have been involved in crime, to follow them up and punish them – this is to entrap the people." Confucius (16: 1) mentions: "I have heard that rulers of states and chiefs of families are not troubled lest their people should be few, but are troubled lest they should not keep their several places; that they are not troubled with fears of poverty, but are troubled with fears of a want of contented repose among the people in their several places. For when the people keep their several places, there will be no poverty; when harmony prevails, there will be no scarcity of people; and when there is such a contented repose, there will be no rebellious upsetting. Therefore, if remoter people are not submissive, all the influences of civil culture and virtue are to be cultivated to attract them to be so; and when they have been so attracted, they must be made contented and tranquil."

We now examine Fukuzawa's thought about economic liberty. Although his arguments were strongly influenced by Western economic theories, we demonstrate that his thought does not deviate from the ancient Confucianism. He stated in his *Autobiography*, "there is nothing more fearful to me than a debt unless, perhaps, it is the shadow of assassination. Ever since early childhood, my brother and sisters and I had known all the hardships of poverty." In his individual behavior as well as in his thought for Japan's civilization, economic development was a key concern.

The quest for profit was considered to be the vice in Japanese Confucian society. It meant putting one's own pleasure and advantage above dutiful consideration of one's place in the family and society.) From traditional political economy, Fukuzawa learnt that there are economic laws in socio-economic life beyond the control of human beings just as there are natural laws in physical phenomena. Like Adam Smith, he held that self-interested is the foundation of public interest and public interest is in turn achieved by the act of people who look after their own profits.) As Kumagai pointed out, "'It follows from this 'fighting for profit is nothing but fighting for *li*' (the natural reason, or principle)....By resorting to the fundamental concept of Confucian learning, *li*, Fukuzawa attempts here to convert negatively perceived ideas of self-interest and profit into positive ones."[8] Like in traditional liberal economics, he believed in that self-interest action would lead to public benefit. (The government should minimize its intervention in economic affairs, except providing public utilities, constructing infrastructure, and fulfilling social capital.) He stressed that free competition must be predominant in domestic economic policy.

Although he did not develop any sophisticated economic theory, his concerns were very broad.[9] In his *Speech What I Ask for the Worlds of Commerce and Industry* in 1884, he pointed out that in Japan there was no nationwide standard for measuring products. Everywhere, "irrational practices" were observed in Japan from nails to stone slabs. These practices confused consumers' eyes and ears. He argued that to establish a prosperous state, "First, we should establish an unchanged and uniform system of measurement for all goods sold commercially. The system of measurement is established by national law."[10] He seems enjoying reading and digesting economic ideas. In a speech made at the Keio Gijuku in 1889, he related what he thought of political economy: "political economy is really fascinating and its refined argument often takes us by surprise. It overturned our inbred Confucian mind."[11] He first published his works on political economy in 1868 in *Seiyo Jijo Gaihen*. He introduced classical political economy based on Chambers's *Educational Course: Political Economy* published in 1852 and Francis Wayland's *The Elements of Political Economy* published in 1837. When asking for his country to "enrich the country and strengthen the army", he emphasized the importance of education in economics. He pointed out that economics explains how to produce economic goods, exchange services and goods, and distribute them. He considered economics a field of human learning that explains that those who follow the natural law become richer and those who fail to adhere to the natural law become poorer. Without knowledge of economics, one could not properly understand the law of being rich and poor.

He was greatly influenced by the ideas of F.P.G. Guizot, H.T. Buckle, H. Spencer, J.S. Mill, S. Smiles, and liberal political economists mainly originating from the British classical school.[11]

From 1859 to 1867 he visited America twice and Europe once as a junior member of government missions and in 1867 he brought home a considerable number of American books including *The Elements of Political Economy* published in 1837 of Francis Wayland (1796-1865). Wayland was president of Brown University and also its professor of moral philosophy. The book was very popular not only in his home country but also in the early Meiji Japan. In his *Autobiography*, he recalled, "It was one of those which I had never before come across. At first I felt it difficult to read it, but after getting used to it by reading it twice or thrice, I was so deeply impressed by every chapter or even every phrase, with its arguments and expressions completely fresh to me, so much so that I often forgot about having meals." He also mentioned an episode when there was a skirmish at the northern entrance of Tokyo between Shogunate guards and the Imperial corps. He continued his lecture on Wayland, ignoring the noises and firing which excited the audience.

Fukuzawa studied economics with Wayland's *Political Economy* and the two books of John Hill Burton's *Political and Social Economy: Its Practical Applications* (1849) and *Chambers' Educational Course: Political Economy for Use in Schools, and for Private Instruction* (1852). The last one was published anonymously and the author was identified recently as Burton. Before reading Wayland's books, he was not very certain about how to replace the traditional Confucian system of morals by a new one suitable for the upcoming bourgeois middle classes as driving forces of the new Japanese society. When one of his students found a copy of Wayland's *Elements of Moral Science* in a second-hand bookshop nearby his school, they studied it enthusiastically to find a new system of morals. Wayland's moral teaching began to be propagated in the forms of translation, excerpts, and adaptation. Although it was nothing more than a modernized version of Christian ethics, the idea that a mutual regard for each other's rights is an indispensable foundation of society was very fresh for those who were educated by the Tokugawa Confucian morals of subordination.[12]

The Western economic liberalism awakened the Japanese who had been long accustomed to living passively under feudal control. The pragmatic response of Japanese liberals who realized the gap between advanced Western nations and their own. He was the forerunner of this movement. Deeply impressed by the basic teaching of the Western political economy, he stressed the independence of individuals and advocated a new moral on the principle of reciprocity that was open to free competition. However, he also realized that a predetermined harmony could not emerge automatically in international trade relations where there existed a discrepancy between the strong and the weak nations, or more precisely, the advanced and the delayed nations.

He held that the nation has to accumulate wealth for it to become independent. Japan should not only admire *samurai*, but also respect commerce if Japan wanted to become independent.[13] When he described how to enrich the nation in his 1879 book, *A General Discussion on Rights of Nations*, he argued that if Japan failed to accumulate wealth and enrich itself, other powerful countries would control the country even if Japan emphasized and protected its international rights, had knowledge about international as well as domestic affairs, and was not interior to any other country in talent and virtue. If it was enriched, Japan would not only make the country beautiful and demonstrate powers, but also went into wars with other countries and won battles. All such glories were due to wealth. If the country had money, it could also produce or buy weapons and maintain armies by employing or hiring soldiers. As the current world was characterized of being unfair, he also argued that one could control public opinions with money.[14] If one had money and controlled public opinions, it would not difficult to defeat enemies. This rule of wars with money, he pointed out, was observed not only in the West but also in Japan in recent years. In order to guarantee the rights of one's nation, it is necessary to develop economy and enrich the nation. Without wealth, the "national rights" would not be sufficient to guarantee the national survival in the unfair international environment.

In *Gakumon no Susume*, he also pointed out that when considering the current state of Japan and enumerating the points in which Japan was falling short in comparison with Western countries, Japan should first consider science, second commerce, then law for the national security and development.[15] As civilization was supported by these three pillars, and when they are not developed, a country could not be independent when the three pillars fell down. To develop commerce, competition should be encouraged. He believed that competition was the basic force of civilization. In *Bunmeiron no Gairyaku*, he discerned the essence and the appearance of the 'civilization' and defined the former as the "progress of the intelligence and virtue of the people". In order to catch up to the advanced nations, the Japanese should not take an easy way, but began with cultivating the sense of independence before Japan was fully attracted to Western products. He held that civilization was the universal course of development among nations, so long as they did not lose their sense of independence.

According to Fukuzawa, progress of civilization is carried out by people and the role of the government is to create an environment for people to pursue their own intentions. Indeed, he was also faced with the fact that western society was motivated by narrow and anti-social self-interested greed, but the result was public wealth and private morality. While Confucian China and Japan were educated with Confucian doctrines, the societies were characterized of dishonesty and private immorality. He observed that Japanese merchants, like Chinese ones, could not be trusted, but Western merchants were trustful and honest. He explained this difference as follows: "Westerners try to expand their business to gain greater profits in the long run. Because they are afraid dishonest dealings will jeopardize long-range profits, they have to be honest....Japanese are greedy on a small scale, foreigners are greedy on a large scale."[16]

He directly related honesty and profits. He found that growing affluence tended to improve private morals. This is actually what Confucius held that improved living conditions enabled people to develop a sense of shame. In the ancient Confucianism, moral symbols are emphasized not only because they might educate directly people, but also because people who even don't have a sense of shame would imitate the socially desirable symbols for their own benefits (or "face"). In the ancient Confucianism, positive interrelations between honest behavior and profits are interpreted even much wider than Fukuzawa.

In *Gakumon no Susume*, he pointed out that in the histories of various countries of the West, commerce and industry were not created by the government.[17] The origins of all developments could always be identified among the innovation of thinkers from the middle class of society. Watt invented the steam engine; Stephenson devised the locomotive, and Adam Smith studied the laws of economics and brought about a change in commerce. All these prominent men belonged to the middle class. When new ideas or inventions were completed in their minds, they formed private companies of friends and put it in practice to promote the scheme further and contribute to the general population and to posterity. The government could play a useful role by allowing this business to progress unhindered. He held that it is the people who actually complete the activities of civilization and the government that supports and protects civilization.

## The Ancient Confucian and His Attitudes Towards Social and Economic Inequalities

Let the people be employed in the way, which is tended to secure their ease, and though they be toiled, they will not murmur.
Mencius (13: 13)

The national power was a main concern for Fukuzawa. He advocated domestic competition and private property. For him, private wealth is also part of national wealth. In *Private Wealth as Public Wealth* in 1896, he argued that it is due to self-interest rather than for  the benefit of the nation that people make efforts to improve productivity and accumulate wealth. Although they are not motivated for the national strength, their efforts actually become the source of national wealth.[18] He held that the authorities should refrain from interfering in the industrial society unnecessarily. To support his arguments, he presented statistical data on export and import items. He also provided a comparison of costs in the textile industry between India and Japan. He pointed out that Japanese products could be competitive against Indian products if the Japanese government abolished its sea route customs, along with its export and import duties.

He believed that man is born equal. But this does not mean that he advocated socioeconomic equalitarianism. He held that inequalities of wealth and status did and should exist. As Heaven created man equally, no one need resign himself to penury and base status fatalistically. Through pursuing practical Western learning, anyone could achieve personal wealth and eminence. Individual growth would bring about national strength and advancement. He insisted that the ever-widening schism between haves and have-nots was a consequence of progress and civilization. In *Words Left in Nakatsu* in 1870, he asserted: "Those who work hard are entitled to appropriate rewards, which is a law set by Heaven, and the reward will be larger for those undertaking difficult tasks....This is perhaps what one would call the law of integrity between the sovereign and the subjects."[19]

In *Gakumon no Susume*, he showed his distrust of ignorant and uneducated for social progress: "There is no one more pitiful and obnoxious than the ignorant and the illiterate....They take advantage of it when they can, yet when their personal greed dictates, they break the law.?"[20] This is similar to what Mencius said: "They are only men of education, who, without a certain livelihood are able to maintain a fixed heart. As to the people, if they have not a certain livelihood, it follows that they will not have a fixed heart. And if they have not a fixed heart, there is nothing which they will not do, in the way of self-abandonment, of moral deflection, of depravity, and of wild license. When they thus have been involved in crime, to follow them up and punish them,—this is to entrap the people. How can such a thing as entrapping the people be done under the rule of a benevolent man? Therefore an intelligent ruler will regulate the livelihood of the people, so as to make sure that, above, they shall have sufficient wherewith to serve their parents, and below, sufficient wherewith to support their wives and children; that in good years they shall always be abundantly satisfied, and that in bad years they shall escape the danger of perishing." Hsün Tze (7: 4) advised what to do for social progress: "Being the worthiest of men, they are able to help the unworthy. Being the strongest of men, they are able to be magnanimous toward the weak. Certainly they are capable of placing others in mortal peril, but they would be ashamed to engage in conflict. With calm solemnity they perfect the arts of civilization and display them to the whole world so that violent states will become peaceful and transform themselves. Only when this has been done and yet some persist in occasioning calamitous portents or remain perversely twisted do they apply the death penalty."

In the ancient Confucianism, inequalities are justified. Nevertheless, it is believed that inequalities have to be kept within certain limits; otherwise, social order may be threatened. In Confucian tradition man is born naturally equal in the sense that each man's social position is singly determined by one's own quality as being human and has nothing to do with any external factor such as family background or race. Confucian tradition holds that economic and ethical elements should have a harmonious relation. In the essay "Equalization" in the *Many Dewdrops of the Spring and Autumn Annals*, Tung Chung-shu (179-104 BC) summarized Confucius' economic principle on the distribution of wealth as follows:

It is said by Confucius, "We are not troubled with fears of poverty, but are troubled with fears of a lack of equality of wealth." Therefore, when there is here a concentration of wealth, there must be emptiness there. Great riches make the people proud; and great poverty makes them wretched. When they are wretched, they would become robbers;

when they are proud, they would become oppressors; it is human nature. From the nature of the average man, the sages discovered the origin of disorder. Therefore, when they established social laws and divided up the social orders, they made the rich able to show their distinction without being proud, and the poor able to make their living without misery; this was the standard of the equalization of society. In this way, wealth was sufficient, and the high and low classes were peaceful. Hence, society was easily governed well. In the present day, the regulations are abandoned, so that everyone pursues what he wants. As human wants have no limit, the whole society becomes indulgent without end. The great men of the high class, notwithstanding they have great fortune, feel bad for the insufficiency of their wealth; while the small people of the low class are depressed. Therefore, the rich increase their avarice for money, and do not wish to do good; while the poor violate the laws every day, and no way can stop them. Hence, the society is difficult to govern well.[21]

In *Li Ki* Confucius set forth his ideas of distribution according to productivity as follows: "To teach the people to make the doing of their duties the first thing, and their salaries an after consideration. A superior man will not for words of small importance receive a great salary, nor for words of great importance a small salary." In Confucian tradition, it is believed that distribution of wealth has an impact on people's minds and thus influences social justice and stability. To maintain a proper distribution of wealth that guarantees each individual a basic living is a kingly way of governing. Mencius said: "This condition, in which people nourish their living and bury their dead without any feeling against any, is the first step of Royal Government." This proper distribution is not enforced equalization but natural distribution under constraints of social justice. Hsün Tzu said: "Where ranks are all equal, there will not be enough goods to go around; where power is equally distributed, there will be a lack of unity; where there is equality among the masses, it will be impossible to employ them." In Confucian tradition, income is not supposed to be equal among all the people since this would result in social declination and economic stagnation; on the other hand, income gaps between groups should not be enlarged "too much" since this would lead to social instabilities and injustice.)

## On Free Trade

Feudal leaders isolated Japan and did not encourage international trade. It was commonly believed in Japan that there was no need to seek more through international trade. (Feudal leaders managed the economy through suppressing people's desires for higher living standards at home and rejecting foreign trade.) But once the door was ajar, the Japanese appetite for "Western things" grew unbounded. "A modern guidebook entry on the port city of Yokohama, near Tokyo, notes that within two decades of the black ships' arrival it boasted the country's first bakery (1860), photo shop (1862), telephone (1869), beer brewery (1869), cinema (1870), daily newspaper (1870), and public lavatory (1871)."[22] In 1862, the Shogunate sent fifteen students to the Netherlands on the first government-approved foreign study program. Thereafter six students were sent to Russia in 1865 and twelve went to England in 1866. The fourth and fifth parties were sent to France in 1867. Various fiefs also sent students abroad during the final years of the Shogunate. After the Meiji Restoration, those wishing to go abroad for study increased considerably. The government first made it a practice to provide reasons leaving the country with travel permits. Soon thereafter it instituted the practice of investigating all travelers bound for overseas, and on February 11, 1871, the Order concerning Study Abroad (Kaigai Ryugaku Kisoku) was proclaimed by the Grand Council. This Order made the University responsible for the program of sending students abroad. In addition to numerous students sent abroad from the Southern and Eastern Colleges of the University, in 1871 a group of five young girls traveled to study in the United States.

In his 1879 *A General Discussion on Rights of Nations*,[23] Fukuzawa advocated free trade. Following the arguments of liberal economics, he held that every country can gain mutual profit by the utilization of its own natural resources and in specifying in specific products suitable to its own country. He accepted the argument that it is the best policy to pursue free trade in order to extirpate the causes of wars. But he did not forget to argue for protectionism. One reason is that if a special product is always imported from other countries, the domestic workers will gradually forget their skills and finally become unskilled in the long term. To secure domestic jobs, he also encourages the government to take action in trade protection. As observed by Komuro, he believed in the classical liberal economic doctrine only as the long-term ideal. As he came to discuss how Japan would benefit from international trade, he argued that this ideal would not be applicable to the Japanese situation. For him, the economic system built by the classical liberal economists was not realistic, but useful as the ideal.[24] He emphasized the necessity in limiting free trade, according to special circumstances. He argued that Japan must protect its manufacturing industries against advanced economies, which would enforce free trade on Japan for their own sake.[25] He regarded protective trade as a sensible and realistic economy for a weak Japan.

In a speech on *The Future of Japan's Silk Industry* in 1896, he analyzed a possible threat from China's silk-reeling industry. He did not see any serious problem at the moment when he was writing as China was producing silk threads with hands. He warned that if China make inventions or import machines and start to produce silk thread suited to international demands, then Japan would be faced with strong rivals.[26] "However, the dull-witted Chinese will progress very slowly. Thus, if the Chinese ever do catch up with us, the world demand for silk will have grown. Therefore, there will be no problem in the area of supply and demand."[27] Many of his ideas about academics, economics and politics are still insightful for understanding contemporary Japan.

## The People's Welfare in Confucianism and His Support for "Enrich Country and Strengthen the Army"[28]

as long as the old retrogressive doctrine of the Chinese school remains at all in our young men's minds, our country can never enter the rank of civilized nations of the world.

Fukuzawa's *Autobiography*

His main concern for Japan was to "enrich country and strengthen the army". Given the special historical conditions when Japan was faced with possibilities of being invaded and colonized by the Western powers, Japan's strategy of "enrich country and strengthen the army" is the same as the general principle of maximizing well-being of the Japanese people in the ancient Confucianism.

Different from the ancient Chinese masters who traveled in different countries and served different governments, he devoted his whole life to Japan's Westernization. He was deeply concerned with the national power in his socioeconomic thought. In *Bunmeiron no gairyaku*, he stated, "Independence of the nation is the purpose." Nevertheless, from the global perspectives, he held that the quest for national independence should be considered as a local cause. In the case of Japan, this was only a local cause of a late-starting nation. For him, the most urgent problem for Japan is to build Japan as an independent country. Without independence from foreign powers, it would impossible to develop Japan to a civilized country. Hence, for him the national independence was equal to the civilization at that historical moment. It was this quest for the independence of the nation that could encourage the Japanese to avoid servility and to demand equality in their transaction with Westerns.[29] In the ancient Confucianism, it is not the national identity but people's welfare that was the goal of social and economic development. It can be seen that he understood well the long-term issues of civilization in the Confucian standard and was explicitly aware of the short-run issues related to national survival under Western powers.

The dominant theme in Confucian political ideology is not ethics. The rationale for the existence of state is not to serve some personalized God or concrete ideology. The state is seen as a mechanism for maintaining moral order and securing people's living conditions. The government is not a means to use people for some special purpose. It is a body of organizations whose end is to serve the people. The ruler's duty is to work for the welfare of the people. Confucius maintains that the best policy of the government is to maintain peace and establish order in society. He proposes five methods—respecting people's business and sincerity, loving people, taxing properly and operating economically—for the government to win the trust of the people and make them contented and tranquil. The people obey the ruler only if the ruler behaves in a proper way. If the ruler fails to behave in just way toward the people, the ruler's authority should be rejected.

In Confucian tradition the essential purpose of government is to promote welfare of the people, but not to serve special interests of any minority, or a special group of power holders. A ruler is good only when he can and will enjoy (suffer) when his people enjoy (suffer). It is the duty of government to provide benevolent policies. On the other hand, it is the duty of people to carry out their tasks. "The people are the most important element in a nation," assures Mencius, "the spirits of the land and grain are the next; the sovereign is the lightest." The duty of the state is not to order people to do what it desires, but to provide people what they desire. The government should behave in such a way that the people's welfare is increased. ("There is a way", Mencius, points out, "to get the empire;—get the people, and the empire is got. There is a way to get the people;—get their hearts, and the people are got. There is a way to get their hearts;—it is simply to collect for them what they like, and not to lay on them what they dislike." We may argue that democracy in modern times is to establish such a government.) Regarding the happiness of the people as the most important business of society and thinking of the love of the people as the way to hold power, Confucian tradition holds that society should not be ruled by force but operated in the kingly way or the way of moral power. "When one by force subdues men," assures Mencius, "they do not submit to him in heart. They submit because their strength is not adequate to resist. When one subdues men by virtue, in their hearts' core they are pleased, and sincerely submit, as was the case with the seventy disciples in their submission to Confucius." Since a good government takes the welfare of its people as the main purpose of governing, society under such a government should attract people from both near and far away. Confucius said: "Good government obtains," judges Confucius, "when those who are near are made happy, and those who are far are attracted." The goodness of the government is judged by its people's happiness and other people's feet. We read from the *Book of Rites*, Confucian classics, "Through the perception of right produced by ceremony, come the degrees of the noble and the mean; through the union of culture arising from music, harmony between high and low. By the exhibition of what is to be liked and what is to be disliked, a distinction is made between the worthy and unworthy. When violence is prevented by punishments, and the worthy are raised to rank, the operation of government was made impartial. Then come benevolence in the love of the people, and righteousness in the correction of their errors; and in this way good government held its course." Once Fan Chi asked Confucius about benevolence. Confucius replied: "It is to love all men". He then asked about knowledge. Confucius said: "It is to know all men." Fan Chi wondered what Confucius meant by these answers. Confucius further explained: "Employ the upright and put aside all the crooked – in this way, the crooked can be made to be upright." Fan Chi still could not understand Confucius and then asked Zixia about what the master meant. Zixia replied: "Truly rich is his saying! Shun, being in possession of the empire, selected from among all the people and employed Gaoyao, on which all who devoid of virtue disappeared. Tang, being in possession of the empire, selected from among all the people, and employed Yiyin, and all who were devoid of virtue disappeared." In Confucian tradition, it is through establishing good tradition and selecting benevolent politicians to important positions that a country can become civilized.

Confucianism, which was created in an agricultural economy where mass education in contemporary scales and transportation and communications in contemporary speeds were beyond rational consideration of ancient thinkers, did not advocate for the sovereignty of the people. In fact, Confucianism had never the idea of the sovereignty of the people. Nevertheless, this does not imply that people's welfare could be neglected by the state. Mencius (4: 14) taught that "The people are the most important element in a nation; the spirits of the land and grain are the next; the sovereign is the lightest." Hsün Tzu (27: 72) expressed the significance of people's welfare in a similar way: "Heaven did not create the people for the sake of the lord; Heaven established the lord for the sake of the people. Hence, in antiquity land was not granted in fiefs of ranked sizes just to give honored position to the feudal lords and for no other purpose. Offices and ranks were not arranged in hierarchical order and provided with suitable titles and emoluments just to give honored status to the grand officers and for no other purpose." In Confucianism, the people's welfare is the sole reason for the existence of government and social ranks are arranged to serve the people rather than any other purpose. According to Hsün Tzu (9: 19), "Why can man form a society? I say it is due to the division of society into classes. How can social divisions be transformed into behavior? I say it is because of humans' sense of morality and justice. Thus, if the sense of morality and justice is used to divide society into classes, concord will result." The Confucian ideal society is hierarchical; this hierarchical system is socially mobile according to principles of morality and justice, rather than birth.

In Confucianism, the goal of the country is the welfare of the people and there is no absolute arbitrator of the truth. People's opinions should be taken into account. Mencius (2: 7) advised the King Xuan of Qi: "When all those about you say: 'this is a man of talents and worth', you may not for that believe it. When your great officers all say: "This is a man of talents and virtue,' neither may you for that believe it. When all the people say: 'This is a man of talents and virtue,' then examine into the case, and when you find that the man is such, employ him. When all those about you say: 'this man won't do', don't listen to them. When your great officers all say: 'this man won't do', don't listen to them. When all the people say: 'this man won't do', then examine into the case, and when you find that the man won't do, send him away." The king of Qi attacked Yan and conquered. When the king asked Mencius about whether he should take of possession of it, Mencius (2: 10) replied: "If the people of Yan will be pleased with your taking possession of it, then do so. Among the ancients there was one who acted on this principle, namely King Wu. If the people of Yan will not be pleased with your taking possession of it, then do not do so. Among the ancients there was one who acted on this principle, namely King Wen."

# 6

## Equality Among Nations and "Leaving Asia"

When right government prevails in the world, princes of little virtue are submissive to those of great, and those of little worth, to those of great. When bad government prevails in the world, princes of small power are submissive to those of great, and the weak to the strong. Both these cases are the rule of Heaven. They who accord with heaven are preserved, and they who rebel against Heaven perish.

Mencius (7: 7)

Being confronted with the danger for his motherland from the powerful West, Fukuzawa "correctly" suggested Japan to "leave Asia" according to the historical conditions.[1] When the Meiji emperor was restored as head of Japan in 1868, Japan was militarily weak, primarily agricultural, and technologically disadvantaged. It was controlled by hundreds of semi-independent feudal lords. The Western powers had forced Japan to sign treaties that limited its control over its own foreign trade and required that crimes concerning foreigners in Japan be tried not in Japanese but in Western courts. Nevertheless, recognizing the weakness of the Qing dynasty and Chinese culture, Japanese had swiftly denied Chinese culture and turned their attention to Western civilization when Japan was faced with challenges from the Western powers. When the Meiji period ended, with the death of the emperor in 1912, Japan had: (1) a highly centralized, bureaucratic government; (2) a constitution establishing an elected parliament; (3) a well-developed transport and communication system; (4) a highly educated population free of feudal class restrictions; (5) an established and rapidly growing industrial sector based on the latest technology; and (6) a powerful army and navy. It had regained complete control of its foreign trade and legal system, and, by fighting and winning two wars (against a major Asian power, Qing China, and an European power, Russia), it had established full independence and 'equality' in international affairs. In a little more than a generation, Japan had had changed its whole society.

In his way to Europe in 1862, Fukuzawa stopped at Singapore where he was informed how Chinese suffered under civilized peoples. As he perceived China as a symbol of semi-civilization, it is naturally for him to suggest to Japanese people that they should avoid China and learn from the Western civilization. For him, Qing China was to be occupied by the Western powers (by the 1870s he might have not been even able to imagine that Japan could occupy some part of China). He was later criticized as a supporter of imperialism because of an essay *Datsu-A Ron* (*Leaving Asia*) published in 1885, as well as for his support of the Sino-Japanese War (1894-1895). In his elderly days, he felt happy to see the Japanese victories over China. He died in 1901, before the Japanese war machine had begun to gain the momentum that would carry it into World War II.

**Complete Westernization**

[A]nyone who opposes it [Western civilization] will be ostracized from the human society; a nation, too, will find itself outside the world circle of nations.
Fukuzawa[2]

In his teaching at Keio Gijuku, through the policy of his newspaper, and in his voluminous and lucid writings, he had constantly shown that traditional Japanese ideas and values were wrong. He was aware of differences between Japan and other civilized countries. He considered it his own duty as a Japanese citizen to be concerned with differences among civilizations and make efforts for Japan's civilization. To save Japan, he strove to prove that Japanese had to accept Western positivism and liberalism. "Transportation has become so convenient these days that once the wind of Western civilization blows to the East," he warned Japanese about the real threat of Western powers, "every blade of grass and every tree in the East follow what the Western wind brings."[3] He pointed that anyone who made a careful observation about what was going on in the world at that time, one should know the futility of trying to prevent the onslaught of Western civilization. He asked why Japan would not float with the West in the same ocean of civilization, sail the same waves, and enjoy the fruits and endeavors of civilization.

He believed that Japan had to be fully Westernized in order to avoid being colonized. He described the movement of a civilization like the spread of measles. He held that there was no effective way to prevent the spread of the communicable disease, even though Japanese people might hate it. Nevertheless, he argued that there was no need to be *Really?* afraid of possible damages brought about with civilization simply because benefits would far outweigh harms. As benefit was much greater than cost, there was no point in trying to prevent the spread of civilization. Moreover, he thoroughly rejected the achievements of Japanese civilization. "If we compare the knowledge of the Japanese and Westerners,...there is not one thing we excel....We think that our country is the most sacred, divine land; they travel about the world, opening lands and establishing countries."[4] He did not think that the contemporary Japan had anything to take pride vis-à-vis the West, perhaps except its scenery. He tried to diagnose its illness and suggest proper therapy. He considered Japanese civilization diseased after centuries of feudal tradition and oppression. All people in Japan, from the administrators at the top down to commoners of the lowest rank were slaves of old customs and traditions. Almost all Japanese people lost individuality and virility. They were capable, intelligent, skilled in crafts. They were also brave when placed in a well-defined position of duty. But they seldom had the country to stand and fight in defense of their beliefs when left alone. Japanese people were good servants of their masters; but they would become helpless when their masters died or were dismissed. For him, this was a collective illness. To save Japan from its endured illness, the only hope was to introduce a new and more powerful spirit. The way was evident – to learn from Western civilization and discard Japanese civilization. There was no other civilization, except Western civilization, that was on the right path toward the correct goal. All other civilizations were either wrong or primitive – they were destined either to extinction or to become westernized. Irrespective of his rejection of his cultural heritage, He did not lose hope of Japan for the future. He believed that progress is universal and any nation can achieve civilization if it follows correct principles.

In 1885, the West had already dominated almost the whole world. He held that it would be useless to oppose the western powers. He admired the energetic and aggressive characteristics of the Western peoples. Western civilization had been succeeding in expanding their knowledge and control of nature and society through the use of science. Without rapid steps toward Western civilization, Japan might become another colonized India or pitiable China. There was no time for Japan to hesitate or waste. Only rapidly spreading the modern scientific way of thinking and independent spirit could save Japan from being colonized. The best way to speed up Japan's civilization, Japan should adapt the Western civilization in all aspects. He knew that there are the short-term and long-term values in civilization. He insisted that national independence was the important goal of Japanese civilization. Japan, like Western nations, should enjoy national independence. In *Bummeiron no Gairyaku*, he reasoned that Japan should promote civilization with a well-defined view. To maintain the spirit of national independence, Japan first of all had to distinguish between Japan and other countries. There was no other way than that of adopting western civilization in preserving Japan's independence. This was the only reason, he emphasized, that he asked the Japanese people to adopt western civilization as rapidly as possible. For him, Japan's independence was the goal and Westernization was a means towards this end. He explained: "People may object that man is destined to aim for far nobler and higher things than merely preserving his country's independence.…It is Japan's present needs and present welfare that I have in mind. I do not pretend to advance an abstruse doctrine of permanent significance."[5]

In his 1884 *Opening or Isolation?*, he discussed two possible policies, opening or isolation, for Japan to choose between. "The opening policy" meant an adjustment of Japan to the Western countries in all respects, while "the isolation policy" was intended to manage everything in a Japanese way. The isolation policy required enjoying equal rights in relation to other countries. This would be a challenge to Western countries, as they had been regarding Asian countries as lower than them. He did not consider it impossible to choose the isolation policy, though it involved a rivalry with the Western countries. Two weeks after his *Opening or Isolation?*, in *We Are Obliged to Follow the Westerners in Religion Too*, he argued that Christianity should not be dangerous to Japan. He thought that as Japanese were obliged to protect themselves by imitating the Western way and Westerners were regarding those ways of life which were different from the West as barbarian, Japanese imitate the West not only in social institutions and manners, but also in religion and other matters so that Westerners would feel it difficult to discriminate against Japanese. He gave the support to the government's decision that Christianity was to become the state religion of Japan. He explained his viewpoint: "The civilized nations of Europe and America have always held that non-Christian countries could not be treated as enlightened nations.…[I]t is absolutely necessary that we remove completely the stigma of being an anti-Christian country and obtain the recognition of fellowship by the adoption of their social colour." He also said: "From the standpoint of a private individual, we may say that we take little or no interest in the subject of religion, as it does not affect our personal feelings or sentiments." As discussed by Koizumi, he did not believe in any religion, even though his concern with religions was continued over lifetime.[6]

He proposed the adaptation of Western ways in all respects. Yonehara gives two reasons for his transformation from "partial" or selective Westernization to Westernization in all aspects.[7] The first reason was due to the changes in the political situation. He expected that in the near future a revision of treaties that Edo government had concluded with Western countries. When the revision was accomplished, foreigners would be all over Japan and it would be difficult to exclude anything Western. In particular, he argued that that it would be appropriate to accept Christianity rather than to reject it in vain. The second reason was due to his thought on *kokutai*. Even if Westernization was inevitable, the national identity symbolized by the unbroken imperial line would still remain. Moreover, for him, what was practically important for Japan was not possible dangers caused by Western influences, but how to differentiate Japan from other Asian countries, especially China and Korea. He had tried to convince Japanese people that Japan should detach from China and Korea. What he had been worried about was how Westerners see Japan and the Japanese: "If Westerners see Japan in relation to China, do they recognize any superiority of Japan to China?"[8] He would not like that Westerners would consider Japan an ordinary Asian country. To make Westerners to appreciate Japan positively, it was necessary for Japan to define Asian nations as 'Others'. In his 1885 *Datsua-ron*, he differentiated Japan from China and Korea in order to enable Westerners to recognize Japan as a civilized nation.

## "Might Is Right" in International Relations

Men are partial where they feel affection and love; partial where they despise and dislike; partial where they stand in awe and reverence; partial where they feel sorrow and compassion; partial where they are arrogant and rude. Thus it is that there are few men in the world, who love, and at the same time knew the bad qualities of the object of their love, or who hate, and yet know the excellence of the object of their hatred.
The Great Learning

"Each individual man and each individual country," Fukuzawa claimed in *Gakumon no Susume*, "... is free from bondage. Consequently, if there is some threat that might infringe upon a country's freedom, then that country should not hesitate even to take up arms against all the countries of the world."[9] As nations are equal, each nation should make efforts to be independent of any other nation. He held this ideal for relations among nations. Nevertheless, in international affairs, he believed in the survival of the fittest. For him, negotiated treaties based on rational discussion had little value in the real world. He believed that "A few cannons are worth more than a hundred volumes of international law. A case of ammunition is of more use than innumerable treaties of friendship....A nation does not come out on top because it is in the right. It is right because it has come out on top."[10]

He appreciated the tendency of Western civilization to head for the realization of equal rights among people. He also believed that the concept of equal rights should be extended to international relations. High civilization must be based on natural and rational principles of equality. In *Gakumon no Susume*, he put Japan and the rest world in the same basis. He held that Japan and Western countries live on the same earth and enjoy the same sunshine. The countries should promote each other's interests and pray for each other's welfare. They should also associate with each other, following the principles of life and nature.

He argued: "We must respect even black African slaves if they have *li* (the natural reason, or principle) on their side....Both individuals and countries possess freedom and independence based on *ten no doli* (the natural reason ordained by heaven)."[11] Here, he used Confucians words, *ten no doli,* to express the real principles of life and nature. Indeed, he was not blind to the realty. He saw that the actual relations in the world did not consist of equal rights among nations. In *Bunmeiron no Gairyaku,* he asked the question of to whom the contemporary America originally belong.[12] The white people drove out the original masters of the country, the Indians. The white people changed the position of host and guest by their forces. The civilization of the American should be considered as the civilization of the white men rather the civilization of America. In *A General Discussion on Rights of Nations* published in 1879, he cautioned Japanese people that in the contemporary world, one would either kill or be killed. This was the *Tao* in reality. The *Tao* was particularly true among nations when no universally moral codes existed and international laws were nothing but decorations printed in papers. All peace talks and agreements among nations were ornamental. He held: "In order to excite hearts of all the people and inspire them within a country, there is no easier method than to fight against a foreign country."[13] He established the personal, national, and global models with the independent spirit; but he did not advocate Japanese people to believe this ideal for interpreting contemporary international affairs in short terms.

In *Words Left in Nakatsu* in 1870, he observed that Japan had been opened to foreign trade and there were at times some foreigners who had tried to make Japan poor and make fools of Japanese by reaping profits for themselves.[14] He emphasized that those who had advocated old Japanese or Chinese studies tended to be the easy victims of these foreigners. He insisted that the only way to defy these foreigners at this historical point was Western studies. Japanese people should read widely in the books of the countries and learn the true circumstances of the world so that Japan would become able to discuss the public affairs of the world in the common language of the world. In particular, Japan should accumulate knowledge and virtues for giving free rein to the independence and freedom of all Japanese citizens. Also in international business Japan should learn to abide by the laws of the world to exalt the independence of the country. In his time, to learn from Western civilization also meant to adapt social Darwinism and nationalism. Toward the end of his *Gakumon no Susume*, he argued that it would be useless to talk about Japanese civilization if there was no country and no people.[15] After analyzing the international conditions, he claimed that Japan's goal of civilization was the country's independence.

He believed that might was right. On the other hand, he also recognized usefulness of rational negotiation under certain circumstances. He held, for instance, that England's conduct in the Opium War was understandable. The Chinese had no idea about the existence of the rational principle between nations, not to mention that China was weak. Chinese were obstinately distrustful of all foreigners. If the Chinese had had reasonable negotiations with England and explained the harmfulness of drugs, England would have no reason to have the Opium War with China. He argued: "As it was, however, the Chinese had violently burned and destroyed the English opium – so that England had reason in plenty to grow angry and wage war on China. 'Nobody in the world blames England. They simply laugh at China.'"[16]

## The Confucian Choice by Foot and His "Leaving Asia

Union is sought with one beyond himself, and with a worthy object – he is following the ruler above him.
*I Ching: Bi*

To choose neighborhood is considered an important way of personal cultivation and social improvement in Confucian education. One of the most well-known old stories both in China and Japan is

"Mengmu sanqian", which tells how Mencius' mother had changed her dwelling sites to find proper neighbors in order to educate her son who late became one of the greatest thinkers in East Asia. Applying this old story in Confucianism to his contemporary national relations, Fukuzawa made his advice to his country to leave Asia and become westernized.

He held that it was unfortunate for Japan to be located near China and Korea: "Japan is located in the eastern extremities of Asia. …Unfortunately for Japan, there are two neighboring countries. One is called China and another Korea."[17] In his first issue of *Jiji Shimpo* in 1882, he argued that while Japan was advancing on the road to civilization, Korea still remained stationary. If Korea was unable to become civilized or defend itself, a stronger nation would have to help Korea in the same way that the Western powers had helped Japan in the past. He did not want to see that Korea was under control of backward China or the Western powers. He hoped that Japan should civilize Korea by teaching it modern ways and protect Korea by sending the military to protect Korea's independence. By 1885, he lost almost any hope for civilizing either Korea or China and published his famous essay "On Leaving Asia".

"It is virtuous manners," Confucius (4:1) instructed, "which constitute the excellence of neighborhood. If a man in selecting a residence do not fix on one where such prevail, how can he be wise?" He applied this idea to national relations. For speeding up the process of civilization, it is fruitful to establish friendly relations with those from whom one could benefit and learn. Confucius also said: "Hold faithfulness and sincerity as first principles. Have no friends not equal to yourself. When you have faults, do not fear to abandon them." He followed the strategy of learning through choosing by the following way: "Fukuzawa challenged his countrymen to turn away from scholars of Chinese learning, arguing that they were so oblivious to world development as to be "little more than rice-consuming dictionaries, and to adopt Western culture."[18]

Fukuzawa held that a nation is foolish because its people are fool, not because the government is corrupt. Only the foolish people support a corrupt and ineffective government. Moreover, he believed that in ruling foolish men who have no incentive to learn, reasoning is not effective. They should be ruled by a show of force. In *Gakumon no Susume*, he portrayed: "A Western proverb says, 'Over foolish people, there is a despotic government.' It is not that the government is despotic of itself, it is the foolish people who bring it upon themselves." [19] He also argued that If Japanese people had no clear mind set, its government would be meddle-minded. If people had no logic in their life, the government should also have no logic view about its morality and international relations.

After he traveled to the West, he believed that national independence would be impossible without the spirit of individual independence. This conviction was enforced when he saw the servile attitudes of the Chinese towards the English in Hong Kong on his way to Europe in 1862. The reality reminded him of that people who had no spirit of independence and self-reliance could not embrace any patriotic mind and felt no shame in obeying foreigners. Later, he found that this lack of independent spirit was not only among the Chinese, but also in Oriental countries by and large under the control of the Western powers. In *Bunmeiron no Gairyaku*, Fukuzawa warned Japanese people that although the white men were only along the coast and had not yet penetrated into the interior part of China, it was very likely that the Chinese Empire would become nothing but a garden for the Europeans in the future. [20] His suggestion that Japan should "leave Asia and enter the West" is perhaps the most well-known rhetorical attempt to dislodge Japan from its former position in the ancient, but changing geo-political East Asian order. He believed: "public and the private sectors alike, everyone in our country accepted the modern Western civilization. Not only were we able to cast aside Japan's old conventions, but we also succeeded in creating a new axle toward progress in Asia. Our basic assumptions could be summarized in two words: *Leaving Asia (Datsu-a)*." [21]

*China?*

He held that Japan and Korea had done nothing for Japan at the moment. Moreover, according to Fukuzawa, "The governments of China and Korea still retain their autocratic manners and do not abide by the rule of law." [22] Because China and Korea are close to Japan, he was afraid that westerners might also consider Japan a lawless society. This bad image was not good for Japan to adopt Western civilization. He pointed out, "It is not different from the case of a righteous man living in a neighborhood of a town known for foolishness, lawlessness, atrocity, and heartlessness. His action is so rare that it is always buried under the ugliness of his neighbors' activities." [23] He further held: "The Chinese and Koreans are more like each other and together they do not show as much similarity to the Japanese. These two peoples do not know how to progress either personally or as a nation.…In this new and vibrant theatre of civilization when we speak of education, they only refer back to Confucianism.…As for their morality, one only has to observe their unspeakable acts of cruelty and shamelessness. Yet they remain arrogant and show no sign of self-examination." [24] With regard to what Japan could do with the two undesirable neighborhoods, he told Japanese people that Japan had no time to wait for the enlightenment of its neighborhoods so that they could make progress together with Japan. It was desirable for Japan to leave the ranks of Asian nations and cast Japanese lot with civilized nations of the West. Japan should treat these two neighboring countries just in the same way as the Westerners treat them.

He despised Chinese and Koreans as poor and backward. In 1883, he argued that as the strong devour the weak, Japan should side with the civilized nations. Likewise, he despised destitute Japanese women and suggested that they work in brothels overseas to earn money and benefit Japan. When he advocated for leaving Asia, he did not mean that the West was perfect. He pointed out: "Robbery and murder are the worst of human crimes; but in the West there are robbers and murderers. There are those who form cliques to vie for the reins of power and who, when deprived of that power, decry the injustice of it all. Even worse, international diplomacy is really based on the art of deception."[25] "Yes, we cannot be satisfied with the level of civilization attained by the West....[Civilization] must pass through sequences and stages; primitive people advance to semi-developed forms, the semi-developed advance to civilization, and civilization itself is even now in the process of advancing forward."[26]

He asked Japan "*Leaving Asia*", basing his arguments on the national utilities. If Japanese could benefit from leaving Japan, he encouraged them to leave Japan. In his speech *Go Abroad* in 1884, he pointed out that America was the most suitable country for anyone to emigrate to. To compare with Japanese, the Chinese emigrated to America and found low jobs. They were looked down by the Americans as dogs and horses. Nevertheless, after a few years hardship, these Chinese return to their home land with a lot of money. "Which of these two races is better?...We Japanese seem to be in an even lower and more embarrassing position than that of the Chinese, whom we refer to as 'those pig-tailed Chinese'."[27] He encouraged educated Japanese to emigrate to America. He argued that as so many Japanese were educated and could not find proper employment at home, to solve problems of over-supplied educated Japanese people, it was desirable for Japan to encourage educated Japanese to emigrate to America. They would eventually become skilled workers because of their accumulated knowledge at home.

## On War and the Sino-Japanese War (1894-1895)

In the *Spring and Autumn* there are no righteous wars. Instances indeed there are of one war better than another. Correction is when the supreme authority punished his subjects by force of arms. Hostile states do not correct each other.
Mencius (14: 2)

"I found one day in school", said Bertrand Russell who had spent a long time in China, admiring Taoism to Chinese audience when China was suffering from wars, "a boy of medium size ill-treating a smaller boy. I expostulated, but he replied: 'The bigs hit me, so I hit the babies; that's fair.' In these words he epitomized the history of the human race."[28]

In *Bunmeiron no Gairyaku,* he pointed out: "Although the Ming and Qing dynasties appear to be similar on surface, the nationality of Southern China of the Ming dynasty had been replaced by that of the Manchu from Northeastern China in the Qing dynasty."[29] When he despised China, he referred the China to the Manchu nationality. Han Chinese had lost their nationality since 1644. He also criticized Chinese imperialism in Korea. In a world characterized of competition over territories, a weakened China occupied a position, which simply did not suit China's international position in the division of global powers. In *Minnzyou Itusin* published in 1879, he pointed out that because of changed international conditions, the Qing China would either be occupied by foreign powers or accept civilization to reform the government.[30] This was the historical current and it was, according to him, impossible to resist. Fukuzawa's belief that China would be occupied by foreign powers was established long before Japan became powerful and when Japan also faced with the possibility of being conquered. In *On Diplomacy* in 1883, he explained international relations: "From the ancient time until today, the way that countries fight each other is like that among beasts....As Japan is nothing but a country in the beast world, she will be eaten up by or will eat up other countries."[31] He held that if Japan did not have power, Japan would be eaten up by or eat up other countries. He recognized that although European countries had made many progresses in civilization and had become enriched in association with advancements in learning and invention as well as rapid development of industry, commerce, military, and other fields, they were still not satisfied. If Japan did not learn from the West, Japan would be soon be invaded by Western powers.

In May 1874, the Shogunate dispatched nearly four thousand *samurai* to the island of Taiwan to punish China for having taken no action against some Taiwan natives who had killed some shipwrecked Ryukyuans. In October of the same year, the two sides held a peace conference in Beijing. The Chinese government admitted that Japan had been in the right side by protecting its own subjects. In addition, China promised to pay a large indemnity to the families of the Ryukyuans who had been killed. In a speech *On The Peaceful Settlement of Taiwan Situation* in 1874, he analyzed: "China…spent millions for useless weapons….[S]he sent 50,000 in money [amounting to 500,000 tales] to Japan in order to secretly perpetrate her crime. This cost her both money and prestige, and she gained nothing."[32] He showed that although Japan's size was only one twentieth of China, the strength of a country did not depend solely on its size. Once Japan determined to fight, Japan was able to maintain its prestige as an independent country without much sacrificing. Although they might feel pity about China's plight, Japanese people should feel proud because the national prestige had been elevated by the victory. He also told that it was also the time to be satisfied as Japan had already enough; but when considering Japan's long-term civilization and the Westerners' behavior, Japan should not be satisfied.

He sensed huge potential profits from China from the Western modern history even long before the Sino-Japanese War. He asked Japan not to lose the opportunities in the future. It should be noted that he was born into poverty and had to struggle with material survival. He described his struggle period: "I often carried out some pretty raw tricks which I rather blush for today. Yet at that time I felt not the least scruple of conscience. Rather, I thought it foolish not to take the money when I could."[33] After his own income was secured and his mind was concerned with the wealth of Japan, he would apply the same principle to a poverty-stricken and weak Japan in the world. As he reminisced in his autobiography, a man's ambition grows according to his position. He had longed to extricate himself from poverty and to become a rich man in Japan. He found his economic conditions secured and he felt he would not be satisfied until he saw his fellow countrymen liberated and the country powerful and rich. He extended his survival logic from his personal level to national level. Even at this time, he did not forget to warn his government that although China should be observed, "it is the cunning Westerners about whom we must be concerned, even during times of peace."[34] He believed that he was living in a time when war decided the prestige of a nation and war decided the prosperity of a nation. He pointed out: "when Napoleon had Europe in turmoil, America's strict neutrality stimulated her production. She exported her goods to Europe and made a handsome profit. Although the conditions of that time were different from those of today, the principle of profiting from the disturbances between other countries remain about the same."[35] He argued that although Japan might not be able to take advantage of the distances among the Western nations, Japan must be careful not to give them the chance to take advantage of Asia. His arguments were not only based on military power, but also based on how different countries managed their economic systems so as to benefit their people as well as nations. China was a "fool" because its government did not accept efficient way to manage its economy. Furthermore, he recognized the implications for encouraging the Japanese spirit: "Our recent victory over China has drastically changed the morale of our people. For the first time, the distinction between home and abroad has been clarified, the basis for our national polity has been solidified."[36] He encouraged Japanese people to build a strong nation by grasping opportunities offered by the heaven. He did not give a certain answer to the future, but asked for people to work hard toward the goal of improving the national welfare. He did not perceive Asia as a real enemy. "Our potential and powerful foes are the Western nations.…The outcome of this battle of wits will depend entirely on the future diligence of our people."[37] He also recognized: "in terms of the moral behavior of individuals, if the hidden reality is examined Western men may turn out to be less ethical, in proportion to the level of their civilization."[38]

In 1881, he published an essay, *Jiji Shogen* (Current Affairs Briefly Discussed), which marked a turning point in this thinking of international relations. It was constructed at the time when the world was filled with wars. The Japanese government, which he supported as contributors to the reforms of the Meiji Restoration and promoters of Western Civilization, was faced with domestic as well as international challenges. In the essay, he suggested that Japan should rely on the power of arms in order to compete with Western nations, saying: "When others [Western nations] use violence, we must be violent too. When others use deceitful trickery, we must do likewise."[39] According to changed situations, he advocated "strength and wealth" rather than "wealth and strength". He urged that for Japan to survive and become independent, the country must put the strengthening of arms first and the enrichment of the country second. He held that only when Japan could succeed in strengthening the government's power and expanding national rights would Japan enjoy a glory of a wealthy and strong nation. In *Leaving Asia* in 1885, he declared: "We must rather break out of the companion and behave in the same way as the civilized countries of the West are doing. We would do better to treat China and Korea in the same way, as do the Western nations."[40] He held that China would be captured by Confucian bonds and would be unable to be civilized. He foresaw that destroying the Chinese (Manchurian) government would be the only way to direct the people towards civilization. It should be noted that the relatively developed Chinese regions, Hong Kong, Taiwan, Singapore, Shanghai and Dalian, were all once invaded by foreign powers and foreign-controlled.

The Sino-Japanese War was a conflict between Japan and China for dominance over China's tributary, Korea. For him, the Sino-Japanese War was a war between civilization and barbarism. Japanese policymakers believed that dominance over the Korean Peninsula by any great power would directly threaten their national security. The Sino-Japanese War was the first of a two limited wars in pursuit of an overarching policy objective. The Japanese expelled Russia from both Korea and southern Manchuria in the Russo-Japanese War (1904-

1905). The first Sino-Japanese War had an enormous impact on foreign perceptions of Japan and China. On the eve of war, the British-owned *North-China Herald* described China as the "only great Asiatic State that really commands the respect of the Great Powers of the World." In less than one year all this changed. Despite China's vastly larger population, army, and resource base, and despite its shorter lines of communication, superior battleships, and years of military modernization, it lost every battle. Its troops fled the field in disarray, abandoning vital supplies, and preyed on the local population. Meanwhile its civil officials focused more on preserving their own power at the expense of their domestic rivals, than on cooperating to defeat the foreign foe. Just as Chinese corruption and incompetence disgusted, so Japanese military prowess and professionalism impressed the war's foreign spectators. Paine relates: "In 1895 the U.S. Secretary of the Navy, Hilary A. Herbert, wrote: "Japan has leaped, almost at one bound, to a place among the great nations of the earth. Her recent exploits in the war with China have focused all eyes upon her, and the world now comprehends the startling fact that this small island kingdom, so little taken account of heretofore in the calculations even of students and statesmen, has within a few decades stridden over ground traversed by other nations only within centuries."[41] The War brought about a new balance of power. China's millennia-long regional dominance had abruptly ended. Japan had become the dominant power of Asia. He could scarcely contain his joy about the Sino-Japanese War: "One can scarcely enumerate all of our civilized undertakings since the Restoration .... Yet among all these enterprises, the one thing none of us Western scholars ever expected, thirty or forty years ago, was the establishment of Japan's imperial prestige in a greater war....When I think of our marvelous fortune, I feel as though in a dream and can only weep tears of joy."[42] The Japanese victory had also confirmed his belief in his ideas about independence and economic freedom. Craig observes, "Victory in war removed the load of Japan from Fukuzawa's shoulders. No longer was it necessary for him to talk up the national spirit or warn the people of present perils."[43]

His support of the Sino-Japanese War had much to do with his opinions about modernization. He believed that China suffered from archaic and unchanging principles. At the time of the war, foot binding was still the practice in China, and political institutions were failing to fend of foreign incursions. In his hopes for a strong Japan, Fukuzawa saw the Asian countries around Japan as potential deterrents in need of guidance. His support of the Sino-Japanese War should also be considered within a global framework with a historical perspective. In *Autobiography*, he did not find any hope for China: "I am sure that it is impossible to lead her [China's] people to civilization so long as the old government is left to stand as it is....they should not hesitate to destroy a government even if it is only for an experiment."[44]

As argued in Zhang, China destroyed its past government (more properly, Manchurian ruling) but has failed to establish a new decent one until today.[45] In *Gakumon no Susume*, Fukuzawa related: "There are some people like the Chinese who think there is no nation in the world except their own, and whenever they meet foreigners, they call them barbarians."[46] He pointed out that since the restoration of imperial rule, the Japanese government had been changed structurally. Japan had also tried to obey international law when was dealing with international affairs. The people were educated or directed to understand the importance of freedom and independence. Common people had been allowed to take family names and to ride on horseback. By the time, the movement to make the four classes – *samurai*, farmer, artisan, and merchant – equal had already been placed on a firm footing. As Toyama argued, it might be unfair to deny all his efforts in civilizing Japan as well as East Asia because he applauded the war.[47] At least, in the historical perspective, he was not wrong as the war had wakened many Chinese people and sped up the collapse of China's last dynasty.[48] "I...was regarding all Chinese culture", he criticized the Chinese culture, "as a mortal enemy. Particularly I despised the false behavior of the Chinese scholars."[49] He argued that China's losing in the 1884 Sino-French War actually helped China because it sparked a sense of independence and a desire for self-help. "In my view, these two countries [China and Korea] cannot survive as independent nations with the onslaught of Western civilization to the East....[W]ithin a few short years they will be wiped out from the world with their lands divided among the civilized nations."[50] He viewed that lost wars provoked backward peoples into accepting civilization and enlightenment – as the 1863 Satsuma and 1864 Choshu defeats had benefited Japan in the long term. Based upon this viewpoint, he justified aggression against the Qing in 1894-5. He did not believe that the Sino-Japanese war would do harm to Chinese people in the long term. He believed that the war was a proof of the power of a united government and people. Through the victory he perceived the strength, wealth and civilization of the new Japan

He did not "despise" any race in the sense that no one or no culture is born into nobility. He did not believe that concrete loyalty like nationalism has any lasting meaning. It is of the nature of medicines to cure mankind of a passing disease. "From the point of view of man's true and perfect nature," he said, "patriotism is merely laughable....[T]his is all nothing more than a necessary remedy for a sick world."[51] Like Confucius, he believed in learning. For him, it is morality and knowledge that distinguishes beasts and human being. Since China had shown no sign of sustainable progress in that time, he asked the Japanese to learn from the West. He did not say that China would be forever anti-progress. The speed of Chinese progress was so slow in his lifetime (the Opium War took place when he was only a boy and the Qing dynasty collapsed soon after he died). During his long lifetime, he had seen nothing about China but one foreign humiliation after another and one domestic destructive rebellion after another. He once said about timing in social evolution: "I have been consoling myself with the thought that when the time comes, society will adjust itself to the needs of the times."[52] When we observe what have happened to China since the economic reform, dimensions of freedom in Chinese society have been greatly enlarged.

Hatred and friendship among nations change more rapidly than we would like to admit. In traditional society, hatred between families might last hundred years. Only a few decades ago, Japan and the US fought in battles and kamikaze made suicidal crash attacks for destroying anything American. The British were prisoners of Japanese. The kamikaze spirit is only a memory for aged Japanese and the American hatred against Japanese may be only kept in the heart of those soldiers or families who had suffered from the direct conflicts during the war. The US, Japan, the UK are now friends in trade and education and allies in fighting for international peace. Mainland China is welcoming foreign investors from those countries, which used military forces to open China's door. Except a few areas in the world  where racial or religious conflicts occur daily, traditional culture matters little in exchanges of goods and ideas and mutual understanding among the rationally educated and enriched nations have achieved a mature level unheard in human history. His *Leaving Asia* was once received with acclamation among Japanese people and now the same idea has almost no appeal to any sensible Japanese. The reason of the reasons that Chinese people has been humiliated in so many ways since he began to write on the spirit of independence had already clearly pointed out by him: "Should our people ever sink into deeper ignorance and illiteracy, the government will become even more severe than it is today. Should people turn their minds to education, acquire an understanding of logic, and strive for civilization, the government will move toward freedom and leniency. The severity and leniency of the government are natural consequences of the worth or unworthiness of the people themselves."[53]

# 7

# Fukuzawa Modernized Manifestations of the Ancient Confucianism

Great perfection seems chipped, yet use will not wear it out;
Great fullness seems empty, yet use will not drain it.
Lao Tzu (6th cent. BC)

The key to understanding a civilization is to examine the visions and thought accepted by its people. To understand Japan and even other Confucian civilizations (including China, Taiwan, Korea, Singapore, and Vietnam), we argue that it is significant to examine Fukuzawa who had systematically modernized manifestations of the ancient Confucianism.[1] In *Bummeiron no Gairyaku*, he asserted: "A discourse on civilization is a discourse on the development of the human mind. It does not deal with the development of the mind of an individual but the minds of people as a group in the whole of society."[2] To appreciate Japan's process of Westernization, it is significant to examine the thinker that Japanese people have mostly respected.[3] It is historically important to note that Fukuzawa had recognized "Western and Confucian teachings [with regard to social order, law, education, and morality] have now grown to one" about one hundred thirty years ago.

It has taken another hundred years for Chinese to notice this convergence. That is the main reason that China has remained, on average, so poor in the world, irrespective of its heritage of Confucianism.

One sees a portrait of Fukuzawa Yukichi on every 10,000-yen note and a portrait of Mao Zedong on the Chinese 100-yuan note.[4] Mao's thought explains "sustained Chinese character" of Mainland Chinese and Fukuzawa's thought provides insights into the collective behavior of Japanese in modern times. It is meaningful to read what Jones warned: "the transformation of China from a model of moral rule to the 'sick man of the east' offered the enticing prospect for additional reflection on the impact of evolution, environment, nutrition and race upon civilization progress and decay."[5]

There are similarities and differences between Confucius and Fukuzawa in thought and behavior. Confucius's father died before he was born and Fukuzawa's father died when he was two years old. They were brought up by their mothers. They did not get proper education in their boyhood – which implies that they were not "polluted" by books. In their boyhood, they were not subject to strict, father-dominated, authoritarian customs at home. They started to study when they were fifteen years old mainly due to self-motivation and curiosity. They were "born" with the love of reading books and learning. When they pursued learning in their early years, they did not think of benefits from learning. They had approached knowledge with free mind. When they were young, they had to do different things in helping their mothers or earning money. They traveled to different cultures and observed different social and economic structures as well as a great variety of customs. They rationally approached the world and had no belief in any concrete religion. Because of their talent, they could establish ideals of society; and because they had traveled to different cultures and had observing minds of reality and hardship for survival, they had a proper sense of reality, in particular, mental levels of the commons and the current situations in societies. They were both living in chaotic international environment when countries were fighting each other without mercy (the "beast world" as Fukuzawa called it). They were married and had children.

They were different in many perspectives as well. Confucius believed, when he was young, that he could improve the world by actual involvement in governments; Fukuzawa advocated that scholars should be independent of the government for promoting civilization. Confucius worked in different countries; Fukuzawa was never employed by any foreign country. Confucius was concerned with self-cultivation; Fukuzawa's interest was concentrated on strengthening and civilizing Japan. Confucius followed the rule that if a country behaved wrongly, men should not serve the wrong course; Fukuzawa asked Japanese people to behave according to the national benefits even if Japan as a nation conducted wrong action towards other countries. For Confucius, knowledge is mainly to understand man; for Fukuzawa, knowledge is natural and social sciences. Confucius advocated for harmony among nations through mutual learning and understanding; Fukuzawa asked for strengthening Japan to join in dividing the world through strengthening country. Confucius believed that the pursuit of truth is the essence of decent human life; Fukuzawa held that the pursuit of learning is nothing but to seriously play one game among hundreds of human games.[6] Confucius believed that his doctrine would last; Fukuzawa valued that his own ideas and thought were useful but not "deep" and would be only "temporary". Confucius was the teacher of his people over centuries; Fukuzawa was "merchant of learning".[7] Confucius was nationwide criticized before China was able to start economic reform; Fukuzawa has been honored by his countrymen who have enriched Japan and advanced science and technology. Fukuzawa learnt from the Chinese classics and despised them in the public as he said in his *Autobiography*: "It is not only that I hold little regard for the Chinese teachings, but I have even been endeavoring to drive its degenerate influences from my country....I know a good deal of Chinese, and I have given real effort to the study of it under a strict teacher....Even the peculiarly subtle philosophy of

Lao Tzu and Chuang Tzu, I have studied after hearing my teacher lecture on them." He was reputed for attacking the Chinese neo-Confucianism and the Japanese Confucianism; but he had never criticized Confucius. His respect for the essence of the ancient Confucianism is expressed by his own words: "my wish is to let Chou Kung's and Confucius's teachings be absorbed into the principles of independence, because this is the time when moral teaching will undoubtedly be changing according to popular opinion."[8]

Fukuzawa is said to exemplify liberalism because he embodied these ideas in his personal life. He is also criticized for supporting policies that were in conflict with the liberal ideas he advocated. Pyle observed: "Fukuzawa…had advocated a modern education and individual rights for women but brought up his own daughters in the strictest orthodoxy." He seems to be in a stage of "rationally learning liberalism" rather than "acting simultaneously according to liberal principles."[9] In a social transitional period, a person tends to behave "inconsistently" with regard to their newly established values and habitual behavior.

"At fifteen," Confucius (551-479 B.C.) portrays his own life, "I had my mind bent on learning. At thirty, I stood firm. At forty, I had no doubts. At fifty, I knew the decrees of Heaven. At sixty, my ear was obedient organ for the reception of truth. At seventy, I could follow what my heart desired, without transgressing what was right." Confucius was mainly concerned with the Way rather than a nation or a culture's survival, while Fukuzawa was mainly concerned with Japan's survival (rather than civilization). It might be argued that Fukuzawa's behavior and thought stopped at those of an excellent imitator as described by Confucius (14: 44) in the following way: "I observe that he is fond of occupying the seat of a full-grown man; I observe that he walks shoulder to shoulder with his elders. He is not one who is seeking to make progress in learning. He wishes quickly to become a man." What Confucius said help us to judge the achievement of East Asia's Westernization in modern times.

## The Ancient Confucianism and His Thought for Open Societies

But should my forebears' words and deed be truly in accord with Confucianism, then I, too, am a believer in Confucianism with no vestiges of doubts.

Fukuzawa[10]

Japan received its higher culture from China for most of the past two millennia. After eagerly absorbing Chinese culture, philosophy, writing and technology for roughly a millennium, Japan almost totally isolated itself for 250 years. Christianity was outlawed, and overseas travel was punishable by death. Japan had been keeping its doors closed to the West since 1639 for fear of the dangerous influence of Christianity on the established social order based on Confucianism. *Really?* However, during this period Dutch merchants enjoyed a monopoly of Japan' foreign trade. Since 1846 the warships of the Western powers successively visited Japanese ports to ask for trade. The Tokugawa Shogunate government started to strengthen its military power. In 1861 it decided to order two warships from an American shipyard, but the Civil War broke out before the end of the year. The order was turned over to a Dutch shipyard in Dordrecht. The following year, for the first time in Japanese history a group of fifteen Japanese was sent by the government to study in the Netherlands. To embrace this new Western culture as desirable, advanced, and superior, the Japanese first rejected East Asian learning as harmful and backward. Nevertheless, if the essence of Confucian civilization was different from modern world, we would be really surprised at how speedily Japan transformed from Confucian civilization into Western civilization since transformation from one type of civilization to another one tends to take long time through experience many destructive structural changes in social, political and economic systems.

There was not much Western learning available to Fukuzawa when he was thinking of the necessity of Westernization and civilization of Japan as well as East Asia. "Fukuzawa's first contact with the West was in 1854 when he began studying Dutch. Five years later he met a foreigner for the first time, and in 1860 went abroad to San Francisco and in 1862 to Europe. His first major book, *Seiyo Jijo*…was published in 1866.…It is truly amazing that Fukuzawa acquired such a vast quantity of knowledge and understanding of Western civilization within such a short time span."[11] Meiji Japanese reformers did not just buy the outward products of Western civilization, such as guns, trains, and ships, in ready-made form, they also wanted to master the inner spirit of that civilization.[12] Fukuzawa played a key role in educating the Japanese nation about the social and economic principles that Westerners used to invent those principles. As this book demonstrated, these principles are Western as well as the principles of the ancient Confucianism.

De Bary observes: "Many twentieth century scholars have tried to identify the 'original Confucius' or interpret the 'Original Analects,' and any number before them in China, Japan, and Korea have tried to do the same.…The search did not end with them and the process goes on; it will never be definitely settled, because the subject itself continues to be endless fascinating and challenging, always open to reexamination."[13] "Communities in danger do not necessarily seek safety in innovation; commonly they reaffirm tradition and cling to it more resolutely."[14] Although Japan's modernization was characterized of denying traditional Confucianism and accepting the Western ideas about civilization and economic liberty, by examining Fukuzawa's ideas and the ancient Confucianism we try to demonstrate what he tried to deny was neo-Confucianism and what he advocated was essentially the ancient Confucianism. As described before, he started Confucian learning when he was fifteen years old. He pursued the studies under the teacher who emphasized the ancient Confucianism. He was proud that he had a good master of Chinese learning. From his writings, one can detect his familiarities with traditional Japanese and Chinese learning. He could have appreciated the essence of the ancient Confucianism also, perhaps, because he started the learning without special social purpose when he was already at a maturing age. His sincerity in pursuing the Confucian classics is important for us to relate his thought to the ancient Confucianism. If he had been taught under a teacher who emphasized neo-Confucianism and learnt with a fixed purpose (to serve his master), he might not have a proper conception of the ancient Confucianism. Although he admired the ancient Confucianism, he criticized neo-Confucianism, the Tokugawa Confucianism, and the Manchu Confucianism. He was well aware of differences between principles and their manifestations. In his article *Questions on Moral Education* in 1882, he observed the differences of Confucian manifestations between China and Japan: "Both the Chou period in China and the Tokugawa period in Japan were feudalistic....These two peoples, who are brought up on the same moral philosophy, react in completely opposite ways in real-life situations. A most surprising phenomenon, but it is proof that a moral teaching, after all, influence people only to the extent tolerated by popular opinion, and not beyond."[15] "Thus in China, the free movement of officials is seen as honoring the precepts of the sages, and in Japan such acts are censured for going against the precepts of the same sages."[16] As the time changed, he argued that it was necessary to adopt the Confucian principles to the changed situations.

By the ancient Confucianism, we mean the Confucian doctrines developed by Confucius, Mencius (371-289 BC), and Hsün Tzu (298-238 BC). The ancient Confucianism was constructed in an era when multiple cultures communicated with, learnt from, and emulated each other. The three ancient thinkers had life experiences in different cultures and served heterogeneous governments. They did not perceive a world controlled by a single government. The world visualized by the ancient thinkers is characterized by harmonious co-existence of multiple cultures. In fact, the commonly perceived Confucianism is referred to the neo-Confucianism adapted for a closed society with some religious favor. Neo-Confucianism was developed long after different countries and cultures had been united into a single China. There was no strong cultural challenge from neighboring countries after the unification until the West opened China's door via the opium war. Neo-Confucianism was developed to serve a united, closed social system with the unchallengeable emperor at the top of social hierarchy.

As an ethical system, Confucianism underwent many changes in the course of history. After the death of Confucius, Confucianism experienced a complicated development process. Having analyzed various schools of Confucianism, I capsule the main Confucian (ethical, political and economic) principles commonly held by the main schools of Confucianism over history:[17] (1) free will and rationality (which lays the foundation for the Confucian regions to be rational, adaptive and progressive and to accept sciences with little cultural conflicts); (2) natural equality and social inequality (which provides the basis for human equality and social mobility); (3) self-cultivation through education and equal opportunity in education (which is the key factor for explaining social appreciation of knowledge and education and emphasis on education); (4) the welfare of the people and the benevolence policy (which provides a sustainable basis for industrialization and democratization of the Confucian regions); (5) hierarchical social structure supported by talent and merit (which is essential for establishing social order according to virtue, merit and education); (6) mutual obligation rather than law in maintaining social justice (which explains why social negotiation cost is relatively high and legal cost is relatively low in the Confucian regions); (7) the rectification of names (which means that one should only get what one is socially or economically 'worth of'); (8) the dynamic operation of market mechanism with government intervention (which implies that the two poles, socialism and capitalism, of traditional rational economic thought hold limited appeal to the Confucian mentality); (9) love with different degrees of intensity (which does not promote "inflation of love" in Freud's term and extreme social welfare in economic sense); (10) respect for hard work and appreciation of frugality (which are important for sustainable economic development); and (11) an emphasis on social harmony and the justification of rebellion against corrupt governments. As discussed in this book, Fukuzawa accepted these Confucian principles.

"The Manchu Qing Dynasty", upbraided Yao, "promoted religious and political Confucianism to an unprecedented high position in history and strengthened the orthodox position of the Cheng-Zhu School on the one hand, and ruthlessly suppressed any new interpretation of Confucian Learning on the other."[18] The Cheng-Zhu School was employed by the Manchus to justify their political monopoly over the Chinese during the Qing dynasty. As early as in 1697, Leibniz described: "The Chinese above all others have attained a higher standard. In a vast multitude of men they have virtually accomplished more than the founders of religious orders among us have achieved within their own narrow ranks. So great is obedience toward superiors and reverence toward elders, so religious, almost, is the relation of children toward parents, that for children to contrive anything violent against their parents, even by word, is almost unheard of, and the perpetrator seems to atone for his actions even as we make a parricide pay for hid deed.…To us, not enough accustomed to act by reason and rule, these smack of servitude; yet among them, where these duties are made natural by use, they are observed gladly."[19]

## The Pioneer of Modernizing Manifestations of Ancient Confucianism

There are the foot-paths along the hills – if suddenly they are used, they become roads; and if as suddenly they are not used, the wild grass fills them up.

Mencius (14: 21)

Fukuzawa is well-known for his assault on Confucianism. On the other hand, he claimed himself to be Confucian in essence. The reader might wonder why he criticizes Confucianism on the one hand, and claimed himself to be Confucian, on the other hand. Like differences between Marxism by Karl Marx and Chinese Marxism,[20] there are different interpretations of Confucianism. The ancient Confucianism is not the same as the neo-Confucianism. The ancient Confucianism was constructed for an open society in an international environment with multiple countries in competition. The neo-Confucianism was the manifestations of the former for an isolated and emperor-centred hierarchical. What he attacked is the neo-Confucianism and what he followed in essence is the ancient Confucianism.[21]

To explain this, we have tried to read and understand the principles of the ancient Confucianism and to examine his basic thought. After these fundamental works, we come to compare the principles of the ancient Confucianism and his thought and ideas. As the two systems are similar in the principles, we can claim that Fukuzawa did modernize manifestations of the ancient Confucianism, even though he might have not done this on purpose. It is in this sense that this book considers him as the pioneer of modernizing manifestations of the ancient Confucianism.

(Hirakawa describes the Japanese features of Westernization in the following way, "In a sense, nineteenth-century Japanese intellectuals needed only to transfer that center from China to the West. In this regard, the Japanese consciousness and problems differed strikingly from those of China, and consequently Japanese thinkers were probably better equipped psychologically for assimilating Western culture than were their Chinese counterparts.")Fukuzawa lived in an era in which Japan had already been prepared for Westernization. The *Charter Oath of 1868* is one of the first documents written by the new Meiji leaders and reveals much about the new society they hoped to establish. The *Charter Oath of 1868* claimed

1. Deliberative assemblies shall be widely established and all matters decided by public discussion.
2. All classes, high and low, shall unite in vigorously carrying out the administration of affairs of state.
3. The common people, no less than the civil and military officials, shall each be allowed to pursue his own calling so that there may be no discontent.
4. Evil customs of the past shall be broken off and everything based upon the just laws of Nature.
5. Knowledge shall be sought throughout the world so as to strengthen the foundations of imperial rule.

Each of the five articles had an important bearing on education. In particular, Article 5 specified the goal of modernizing national education through introducing modern Western civilization. Article 3 indicated a desire to broaden the base of educational policy beyond the traditional elite. The new government adopted the policy of developing education based on the concept of Civilization and Enlightenment.

He devoted his life to speeding up and laying a theoretical foundation for the socioeconomic structure changes. Over his lifetime, books and articles flew from his pen in a steady stream. His concerns ranged widely from the shortcomings of the old learning and new values and new principles. He covered topics in ethics, politics, economics, historiography, international law, and the philosophy of science. He emphasized the spirit of independent observation and criticism, pointed out that the old Confucian system of ethics could no longer promote any positive role in civilizing Japan, and attacked the old family system. Many of these ideas are now taken for granted. But these ideas were published more than one hundred years ago when Japan was just opened to the West. His unique character among the Japanese intellectuals is not his denial of Confucianism, but his belief in individual and national independence even since the early years when he met with the Western civilization. When Japan was forced to open its door in the mid-nineteenth century, he served Japan as one of the most outstanding interpreters and educators of Western civilization. His widely ranged interests from Western philosophy, economics, moral science, new techniques to political institutions and daily life have inspirited the Japanese mind in varied ways even till today. As the father of public speaking in Japan and the most popular writer in his time, no other Japanese had so successfully spread Western civilization on Japanese soil. He was also the founder of Keio University and an influential newspaper, through which he had effectively educated Japanese people in different levels. His influence was beyond Japan – how Korean and Chinese thinkers had been influenced by his ideas before World War II still remain to be examined systematically.

In terms of power, feudal Japan was vulnerable to the Western power. It had not sufficient power to confront challenges from the West. What he was concerned with was not only the rudiments of gunnery for Japan, but also the attitude, which had generated the guns in the first place. Clearly, without such an attitude, Japan would have remained "third world", like Mainland China is still. In a sense, he had planted the "right seed" in Japan's modernization, even though modern Japan might not have grown a perfect plant out of the seed. "Fukuzawa Yukichi taught the Meiji Japanese to learn from the West", Tsuzuki summarizes the pursuit of power in modern Japan from 1825 to 1995, "not only its industrial and institutional skills but, more importantly, the spirit behind its material achievements. The emphasis he places on the independence of an individual, however, did not last long, even with Fukuzawa himself."[22]

He was a passionate believer in the inevitability and value of social and economic progress brought about by scientific advances toward a state of civilization. He saw the nation-states of the contemporary West as the fore-front of world civilization. He seems to have valued the strivings of individuals in Japan not so much for the sake of individual happiness as for their contribution to national progress and strength. This "bias" might come from that he was constantly afraid of possible damages done to his country by the West. He believed that Western civilization and its spirit were valid and applicable everywhere. He argued that Westerners might have discovered these first, but any people could catch up. On the other hand, he never perceived the Western civilization as a perfection of human race. He had encouraged Japanese people to wholeheartedly embrace Western civilization not because he failed to identify the long-run tendency of Western declination, but because he recognized imperfection of common people in learning and perfecting themselves. "As you know," he once confessed in 1869, "I've always been a heavy drinker. But lately I've been reading Western books and thinking about the meaning of life and work....I now see how shameful drinking is, and limit myself to one or two bottles a night."[23] But he also fumed, "Who said whites are civilized? They're beastly white devils....Big-shot ministers and consuls of the civilized British state don't just ignore countrymen who rape [wives of our officials], they aid and protect thee criminals, and so oppress our land, Japan."[24]

Over years, it has been commonly believed that he was anti-Confucian. His essay *Leaving Asia* demonstrates his full acceptance of Western civilization. This book challenges this common perception by demonstrating that his basic vision and thought had no conflict with the principles of the ancient Confucianism. Japan could have accepted and successfully applied his thought and have rapidly become industrialized mainly because he had timely modernized manifestations of the ancient Confucianism. Recognizing his thought within the framework of the ancient Confucianism, one might understand the social and economic principles based on which Japan has been so successful in industrialization and sustainable economic development. This book systematically examines what Fukuzawa meant by "I…am a believer in Confucianism" and why Japan has still honored the man even since he published his first influential book on Western civilization.

"Culture is then properly described," Mathew Arnold depicts, "not as having its origin in curiosity, but as having its origin in the love of perfect: it is a study of perfection." Fukuzawa is reputed for his "pragmatic wisdom", but not for his consistency in principles and ideals. His thinking is not constructed for abstract or ideal, but for civilizing Japan and raising Japan's international status to the same level as that enjoyed by the civilized Western countries. "At one end of the spectrum is a view that regards Fukuzawa as an advocate of autocratic enlightenment, and at other as a civil liberal. Even where appraisal is confined to Fukuzawa's economic thought, it has been called 'a system of miserable contradictions'.[25] Contemporary scholars find faults with his opinions and actions regarding Japanese national strength and expansion, Asian neighboring countries, education, woman, and his dichotomous views on class. His views on education, women, and the class system were not enlightened by today's standards, but for his day they were advanced. Kumagai explains his thought as follows: "The diversity of estimations regarding Fukuzawa can be better understood when one realizes the fact that his writings fundamentally lay in proposing prescriptions for dealing with the problems surrounding Japan in the late nineteenth century....Fukuzawa had to tackle two main tasks: first, the destruction of feudalism and Confucianism ...; and second, accepting Western civilization as a means of retaining the independence of the country.... These two tasks contain contradictions such as individuals filled with independent spirits vs. a strong nation, the people's rights vs. the state's rights, and the idealized Western civilization vs. the factual one."[26] It should also be remarked that Fukuzawa was familiar with not only Confucian learning, but also other Chinese thought, not to mention Japanese intellectual traditions. Intellectually, he did not follow "linearized" traditional Western (Newtonian) way of thinking. If we neglected East Asian cultural influences, he only appears to be a clumsy student of Western knowledge. But if we consider the influence of Shintoism, the *Book of Change*, Taoism, as well as Confucianism, one may judge him differently.

In his time, some Japanese intellectuals held that Chinese learning was still useful but one should not mention it because anything Confucian might "confuse" people (who were using the West as the symbol of power, knowledge, progress, and civilization). For instance, Nishimura Shigeki (1828-1902),[27] educator and moralist of the early Meiji period and author of more than 130 books and 200 articles, an influential official around the emperor, once stated: "Especially the Four Books...can be said to be so far the best teachings in the world....When the Confucian Way is used, its spirit alone should be taken, and I hope the name Confucianism will not be used. The name Confucianism has for some time been disliked by the people, so that there are many who would not believe in the substance because of the name."[28] Nishimura also found fault with Confucianism as a comprehensive and universal doctrine and for its lack of spirit of progress, but he held that it formed the basis for a code of moral values that could serve modern Japan. He followed this attitude towards the ancient Confucianism as well. "It was the old perfection," observed Blacker, a Western expert on Fukuzawa, "in short, towards which Fukuzawa recommended a new road – and one which at first sight appeared a good deal more roundabout. The Confucianist had, after all, hoped to achieve this perfection within the span of a single lifetime."[29]

This book shows that Fukuzawa is important not only for understanding the modern Japan, but also for studying modernization of other Confucian regions (including mainland China, Koreas, Taiwan, Singapore, and Vietnam). The reason (already indicated in the title of this book) is that he is the first intellectual who had systematically modernized manifestations of the ancient Confucianism according to the time. Nevertheless, he failed to achieve what Confucius considered the most difficult. Schopenhauer argues: "In art only the inward significance is of importance; in history the outward. The two are wholly independent of each other... An action of the highest significance for history can in its inner significance be very common and ordinary." We have seen that Fukuzawa's main concerns are "outward". Confucius (5:27) shows the limitation of the most influential Japanese intellectual as follows: "It is all over! I have not yet seen one who could perceive his faults, and inwardly accuse himself." Moreover, man's greatness lies in his creativity. Genius determines the height of a culture. I cite Wittgenstein to illuminate my purpose of examining Fukuzawa and the ancient Confucianism

It might be said that civilization can only have its epic poet in advance. Just as one can only foresee one's own death and describe it as something lying in the future, not report it as it happens. So it might be said: If you want to see the epic of a whole culture written you will have to seek it in the works of its greatest figures and hence see it at a time when the end of this culture can only be *foreseen*, for later there is no one there any more to describe it.

We are now observing the height of Japanese civilization under the influence of Western "determined" by Fukuzawa; and Chinese civilization in modern times will show its height determined by Confucius in the future.

# *Notes*

## Preface

Drucker (2001: 5). [2]  Blacker (1968: xiv).

[3]  Chamberlian (1904: 365).

[4]  As far as I know, there are only two exceptions, Hopper (2005), an excellent biography about Fukuzawa, and Tamaki (2001), a comprehensive book focused on his ideas and behaviour related to economic and business matters. Indeed, there are a number of books in Japanese about Fukuzawa. This book is different from most of the previous studies in that it examines Fukuzawa's thought from the perspectives of the ancient Confucianism.

[5]  Piovesana (1997). This is a difficult task as to understand his thought and personal life, one need not only to know many things related to the Western and Japanese civilizations, but also to know Chinese thought, history, and language(s). In particular, ancient Chinese thought is essential for understanding his thought as a whole.

[6]  Howell (2000).

[7]  Zhang (1999) examines ancient Confucianism and neo-Confucianism. In "the contemporary economic terminology", Zhang holds that the ancient Confucianism is "suitable" for political competition, while the neo-Confucianism tends to be used for "justifying" political monopoly. Zhang (2000) compares political and

economic implications of Adam Smith's thought and the ancient Confucianism. Zhang (2003, 2007) also shows how the ancient Confucianism can be applied to provide some insights into the dynamics of modern (democratic) civilizations.

[8]     Zhang (1998) shows how Japan had followed the ancient Confucianism in its modernization and how China had been against the ancient Confucianism in modern times before the economic form.

[9]     In his 1878 letter to Nakamura Ritsuen (Fukuzawa, 1985: 113). By ancient Confucianism, in this book, we mean the Confucian doctrines developed by Confucius, Mencius (371-289 BC), and Hsün Tzu (298-238 BC). In the literature of Confucianism, the term "classic Confucianism" tends to omit Hsün Tzu's doctrines. See Zhang (1999) for the ancient Confucianism.

## 1  The Pioneer of Modernizing Manifestations of the Ancient Confucianism and Japan's Westernization

[1]     Blacker (1969: xii).

[2]     Blacker (1969: 138).

[3]     The topic is examined in detail by Zhang (1999, 2003). Patten (1999: 164), the last British governor of Hong Kong, observes: "In order to use Confucianism to justify unswerving obedience to the state, you have to turn a blind eye to many passages in the *Analects* that endorse personal liberty."

[4]     *Questions on Moral Education* published in 1882 (Fukuzawa, 1985, 159-61).

[5]     As far as I know, in the last hundred years no influential Chinese intellectual in Mainland China appreciates the essence of ancient Confucianism like Fukuzawa.

[6]     Fukuzawa (1988: 121).

[7]     Kumagai (1998: 26).

[8]     Hill (1972).

[9]     Different from Huntington (1996), who deposits the United States, France and Italy into the same civilization, and Japan and China into different ones, I classify China, Korea and Japan into the same

classification. It should be noted that when discussing civilizations, we should consider adaptation of Communism in mainland China and North Korea an integrated part of East Asia's Westernization.

## 2  Life, Learning and Social Activities

[1]    See Zhang (2000) for comparing Confucius and Adam Smith. Zhang shows that as far as the principles are concerned, Confucius and Smith held similar socio-economic principles; but when they came to issues related to human sentiments, they were different. This book shows that Fukuzawa's ideas are quite Confucian, but his "sentiments" are of Smith.

[2]    Fukuzawa (1985: 113).

[3]    Fukuzawa (1899: 290).

[4]    Fukuzawa (1899: 10-11).

[5]    Fukuzawa (1899: 296-7).

[6]    Fukuzawa (1899: 43).

[7]    Fukuzawa did not mention whether he had ever carefully examined the book, but he had kept the book.

[8]    See Tamaki (2001: 44).

[9]    Tamaki (2001: 43).

[10]  Nagata (2003: 28-30) also mentions close relations between Chinese learning and Fukuzawa's late achievements.

[11]   Nagata (2003).

[12]   Tamaki (2002: 42-3).

[13]   Fukuzawa (1985: 113). Nakamura Ritsuen was a noted scholar of the old school in the Kyoto-Osaka area and had been a close friend of the Fukuzawa family since Fukuzawa's father time. To Fukuzawa, he was like an uncle. In 1878, Ritsuen regarded Fukuzawa as the most noted scholar and educator of the new age. The correspondence between the two was on moral education published in a periodical of the Ministry of Education, and it provoked discussions among the scholars in Japan. The public discussions stopped when the Imperial Rescript on Education was issued in 1890.

[14]   Hirakawa (1998: 36). Sugita Gempaku (1733-1817) was

Physician and scholar of Dutch learning. In 1769 he succeeded his father as personal physician to the daimyo of the Obama domain (now part of Fukui Prefecture). As he related in his book *Rangaku kotohajime*, in 1771 he was invited to witness the dissection of the body of a female criminal executed in Edo and compared his observations with the *Onleedkundige Tafelen* (1734, Anatomical Tables), a Dutch translation of the German work Anatomische Tabellen (1722) by Johann Adam Kulmus (1689-1745). He began the following day to translate it into Japanese, aided by some others. Published in 1774, this translation, entitled *Kaitai shinsho* (New Book of Anatomy), aroused great interest in Western scientific knowledge and methods as the first Japanese translation of a European medical work.

[15]  See Hirakawa (1998).

[16]  Hirayawa (2002: 37).

[17]  Hirakawa (1998: 42)

[18]  Fukuzawa (1899: 22).

[19]  Blacker (2000: 3).

[20]  Fukuzawa (1898: 91).

[21]  Kitaoka (2002: 47). The actual time was 2 years and 9 months as he had to go back home to see his sick mother during the period.

[22]  Hirakawa, (1998: 45).

[23]  Yumiko Miyai: http://www.yomiuri.co.jp/45th-e/45th_08b.htm.

[24]  Fukuzawa (1898: 98).

[25]  It seems that there were only two English teachers available to him, one being good at speaking and the other at reading. See Kitaoka (2002: 59).

[26]  Tamaki (2001: 43).

[27]  Yumiko Miyai: http://www.yomiuri.co.jp/45th-e/45th_08b.htm.

[28]  Fukuzawa (1889: 111).

[29]  Fukuzawa (1889: 112).

[30]  Fukuzawa (1898: 114).

[31]  Tamaki (2002: 49). Fukuzawa had given 100 *ryo* to his mother out of the total 400 *ryo* he received as an allowance from the *bakufu* before his departure.

[32]  Tamaki (2002: 61).

[33]   Hirakawa (1998: 58).

[34]   Different from the popular Western doctrines in Fukuzawa's time, Confucianism is characterized of perceiving the society as an integrated whole. His training in the ancient Confucianism perhaps explains his way in observing and explaining Western civilization. The reader will see this viewpoint as I explain Confucianism in detail in the coming chapters.

[35]   Fukuzawa (1985: 40).

[36]   See *Afterword* in Saucier and Nisikawa (2002).

[37]   See *Explanation* in Komuro and Nisikawa (2002).

[38]   The Freedom and People's Rights Movement (Jiyu Minken Undo), also called the Popular Rights Movement, was a nationwide political movement of the early Meiji period (1868-1912) involving loosely allied dissident groups composed of former *samurai* (*shizoku*) and commoners (*heimin*) whose primary goal was to reform the new Meiji government along Western democratic lines.

[39]   After the Tokyo Earthquake of 1923, financial management deteriorated, and the newspaper was absorbed in 1936 by the *Tokyo Nichinichi Shinbun* (now the *Mainichi Shinbun*). It was revived in 1946 and published for nine years before being absorbed in 1955 by the *Sangyo Keizai Shimbun* (now the *Sankei shimbun*).

[40]   See Nishikawa (1993).

[41]   Fukuzawa was not an original and systematic thinker. His ideas can be found in multiple sources in different languages. The fundamental vision and many of his basic ideas, as argued in this book, are of ancient Confucianism. He seems to be strongly influenced, except many others, by a now almost unknown American educator Francis Wayland (1796-1865). Fuziwara (1993) shows how Fukuzawa was influenced by Wayland.

[42]   Tamaki (2002).

[43]   Tamaki (2001: xxiii). Tamaki examines Fukuzawa's business activities.

[44]   Kiyooka (1985: 16).

[45]   Tamaki (2002: ii).

[46]   See Nishikawa (2001).

[47]   Fukuzawa (1899: 289).

## 3  Civilization Built on Equality, Independence and Learning

[1]    *Questions on Moral Education* published in 1882 (Fukuzawa, 1985: 159-61).

[2]    The "bizarre combination" of Karl Marx and Adam Smith is called "Chinese socialism" in the official documents in Mainland China.

[3]    Kiyooka (1985: 66).

[4]    Kiyooka (1969: 73).

[5]    Kiyooka (1985: 36).

[6]    Blacker (1969: 73).

[7]    Blacker (1969: 74).

[8]    Blacker (1969: 77).

[9]    Blacker (1969: 79).

[10]    This section is based on Chap. 2 in Zhang (2003).

[11]    McClosky and Zaller (1984: 80).

[12]    Zhang (1998).

[13]    As argued in Zhang (2008), mainland China was poor in the last century until the economic reform mainly because the Chinese had been against what Hsün Tzu suggested more than two thousand years ago. From the cultural perspectives, China's economic reform can be, at least partially, interpreted as adapting ancient Confucianism to modern world.

[14]    Lu (1997: 347).

[15]    Kiyooka (1985: 36).

[16]    Blacker (1968: 73).

[17]    Blacker (1968: 73).

[18]    From *Gakumon no Susume* (Fukuzawa, 1985: 68).

[19]    *The Classical of Filial Piety* (1998: 7).

[20]    The discussion on the fair reciprocity is based on Zhang (1999).

[21]    Lu Xun (1980 IV: 29).

[22]    Further discussion on symmetry relations in Confucianism is referred to Zhang (1999, 2003a).

[23]    Howland (2002: 34).

[24]    Blacker (1968: 62).

[25]    Blacker (1968: 63).

[26]    Fukuzawa (1875).

[27]    Nishikawa (1993: 7).

[28]    Chen (1911). See also Chapter 7 in Zhang (2000), where Adam Smith and Confucius's ideal man and ideal society are compared.

[29]    From *The Great Learning.*

[30]    Aizawa Seishisai begins his narrative of *New Theses* [*Shinron*] as follows: "Our Divine Realm is where the sun emerges. It is the source of the primordial vital force sustaining all life and order. Our Emperors, descendents of the Sun Goddess, Amaterasu, have acceded to the Imperial Throne in each and every generation, a unique fact that will never change. Our Divine Realm rightly constitutes the head and shoulders of the world and controls all nations." See Yonehara (2003).

[31]    Yonehara (2003). The following discussion on *kokutai* is based on Yonehara's paper.

[32]    Fukuzawa considered the unbroken imperial line as "a stupid fiction" in the *Bunmeiron no Gairyaku.*

[33]    Yonehara (2003).

[34]    Yonehara (2003).

[35]    Tsuzuki (2000: 97).

[36]    See Fukuzawa (1985: 147).

[37]    Fukuzawa (1985: 134). The essay also plays an important role at the end of World War II when Japan was under the supervision of the Allied Forces. It is imperative that Japan provides a reasoning for the conform between its emperor system and the spirit of democracy. By that time, the emperor was puzzled and consulted his prime minister, who failed to clearly provide an answer. The prime minister was advised to read Fukuzawa"s essay. The essay also opened the emperor's mind. The present order of the Imperial Household was thus formed.

[38]    Fukuzawa (1985: 134).

[39]    Fukuzawa (1985: 134).

[40]    Fukuzawa (1985: 139).

[41]    Fujitani (1989: 73).

[42]    This issue is addressed in Chapter 5 in Zhang (2000).

43    Oxford (1970: 290).

44    See Howland (2002: 106).

45    Mungello (1977).

46    This part is based on Chapter 6 in Zhang (2000).

47    Smith (1759: 341).

48    Smith (1759: 161-2).

49    Smith (1759: 86).

50    Smith (1759: 226).

51    Smith (1759: 25).

52    Zhang (2000).

53    Gordon (1992: 98).

54    Blacker (1969: 63-4).

55    Blacker (1969: 64). This sentence is an echo of Mencius's assumption that human nature is good.

56    Blacker (1969: 65).

57    Fukuzawa (1985: 70).

58    Fukuzawa (1985: 97).

59    Fukuzawa (1985: 89).

60    Even in contemporary Japan, the proportion of leaders who receive higher education in the West in political and business world is very low in the Japanese leaders. This is different from Hong Kong, Singapore, Taiwan, and Korean societies.

61    Fukuzawa (1985: 94).

62    Fukuzawa (1985: 89).

63    Fukuzawa (1985: 91).

64    Nishikawa (1993).

65    Here, we introduced his main viewpoints on gender issues. As pointed out by Nisizawa (2003) in *Explanations*, Fukuzawa was not consistent on some issues related to Japanese reality, such as concubines, over his lifetime. Nevertheless, his ideals do not vary much over time.

66    Fukuzawa (1985: 108).

67    Fukuzawa (1988: 37).

68    Englander (2002).

69    Fukuzawa (1988: 78).

70    Nishikawa (1993).

## 4  Learning, Education and Confucian Meritocracy

[1]    Blacker (1969: 54).

[2]    Zhang (1998).

[3]    Fukuzawa (1985: 70).

[4]    In China, the emperor was engaged in almost all main decisions about national affairs; but as mentioned before, Fukuzawa held that the emperor should play a role of social symbol rather than decision-makings.

[5]    Leibniz (1994).[6]    Shen (1998).

[7]    Shen (1998).

[8]    Montesquieu (1748: 279).

[9]    See Introduction to Montesquieu (1977: 25) by Carrithers.

[10]    Hegel (1991: 138). It should be noted that Hegel's descriptions were based on the information from missionaries. The Chinese in Hegel's book appear to be merchants in South China. Indeed, the spirit of servility was 'universal' in China. But differences in character were great among regions. The farmer in inner land under the Manchu control who had never met with strangers and lived in the same village over generations was different from the merchant in coastal areas who lived under Western influences and far away from the Manchu master.

[11]    Hume (1994: 66).

[12]    Tocqueville (1835: 22).

[13]    Montesquieu (1748: 124).

[14]    Nishikawa (1993).

[15]    Fukuzawa (1985: 124-5).

[16]    Oxford (1970).

[17]    Miyakawa (2000: 11).

[18]    This part is based on Zhang (1999).

[19]    Weber (1951).

[20]    Kiyooka (1985: 17-8).

[21]    Blacker (1969: 54).

[22]    Takami (2001) provides a comprehensive study on this issue in English. The literature in Japanese is voluminous.

[23]    Oxford (1970: 296).

[24] Oxford (1970: 322).

[25] See Hopper (2005: 114).

[26] Hopper (2005: 113).

[27] Blacker (1968: 51).

[28] Kiyooka (1985: 67).

[29] Nakayama (1985: x).

[30] Zhang (2003: 48). This section is based on Chapter 2 of the same book.

[31] Cook and Rosemont (1994: 76).

[32] In his 1878 letter to Nakamura Ritsuen (Fukuzawa, 1985: 113).

[33] Tooyama (1998: 56).

## 5 Competition and Economic Development

[1] Sagers (2006) examined the intellectual foundations of these revolutions, studying the development of *Satsuma* economic thought that overcame traditional Japanese Confucian moral bias against commerce. Sagers' study challenges the standard view that after 1868 Japanese leaders drew inspiration almost exclusively from Western economic ideas and methods. It should be noted that Zhang (1998) studies possible relations between Confucianism and Japan's modernization and Sagers examines the influences of Confucianism on Japan's modernization by examining the history.

[2] Sagers (2006:1).

[3] Sagers (2006:2).

[4] Yagi (2003).

[5] Kiyooka (1985: 66-7).

[6] Nishikawa (2001).

[7] See Zhang (2000). Different from Japan, free competition in official positions through education had often been practiced in China till the time when Japan began to practice social status change through education.

[8] Kumagai (1998: 29-30)

[9] A comprehensive and systematic explanation on Fukuzawa's economic thought is given by a well-known economist in Japan,

Chigusa (1994). His *Fukuzawa's Economic Thought* examines the development of Fukuzawa's economic ideas under rapidly changing socioeconomic conditions. See also Fuziwara (1998).

[10]   Oxford (1970: 324).

[11]   Kumagai (1998: 29).

[12]   Kumagai (1998: 29).

[13]   Hiroshi (1999).

[14]   See his *Respect Commerce in Strengthening the Country* (Komuro, 2003: 267-88).

[15]   Terasaki (2003: 185).

[16]   Macfarlane (2002: 223).

[17]   Fukuzawa (1985: 86).

[18]   Fukuzawa (1985: 97-8).

[19]   Haltutori (2003: 190-1).

[20]   Fukuzawa (1985: 40).

[21]   Chen (1911).

[22]   Fukuzawa (1985: 71).

[23]   The Economist, July 10, 2003.

[24]   Terasaki (2003: 186-8). As Sugiyama (1986) has observed, Fukuzawa's view points on free market varied according to situations.

[25]   See *Explanations* in Komuro (2003: 372-3).

[26]   Kumagai (1998: 31).

[27]   It took more than one hundred years for China to do something with he was concerned.

[28]   Oxford (1970: 345).

[29]   The Confucian ideal government is based on Zhang (2003a).

## 6  Equality Among Nations and "Leaving Asia"

[1]   This correctness is measured in the ancient Confucianism.

[2]   From *On Morality* in 1885 (Fukuzawa, 1988: 79).

[3]   Fukuzawa (1985: 85).

[4]   Craig (1968, 120-121).

[5]   Blacker, (1968: 68).

[6] Koizumi (2002) examines Fukuzawa's attitude towards different religions over his lifetime. Fukuzawa considers religion from the viewpoint of "utilitarianism". Different from Karl Marx who considered religion as opium of people, Fukuzawa said: "religion is like tea" (Koizumi: 2002: 240). In general, he did neither advocate nor criticize practice of religion. He considered religion as a "useful tool" for managing society. As with any other important issues, his viewpoints with special religions, such as Buddhism and Christianism, varied over time, even though his "general" attitude toward religion remains little changed.

[7] See Yonehara (2003). It should be noted that Fukuzawa did not hold that all traditional aspects of traditional Japan were undesirable (see Sakamoto, 2002: 299-312).

[8] Yonehara (2003).

[9] Nishikawa (1993).

[10] Hopper (2005: 120-1).

[11] Kumagai (1998: 26).

[12] Kumagai (1998: 26).

[13] Terasaki (2003: 201).

[14] Fukuzawa (1985: 41).

[15] Tsuzuki (2000: 79).

[16] Tsuzuki (2000: 79).

[17] Fukuzawa (1885).

[18] Hirakawa (1998: 62).

[19] Fukuzawa (1985: 71).

[20] See Kumagai (1998).

[21] Fukuzawa (1885).

[22] Fukuzawa (1885).

[23] Fukuzawa (1885).

[24] Fukuzawa (1885).

[25] Fukuzawa (1875).

[26] Fukuzawa (1875).

[27] Oxford (1970: 336).

[28] Source: *Education and the Social Order* from http:// www.wisdomquotes. com/cat_education.html.

[29]   Tozawa (2002: 40).

[30]   Komuro (2003: 65).

[31]   Iwatani and Nisikawa (2003: 291).

[32]   Oxford (1970: 307-9).

[33]   Fukuzawa (1899: 276).

[34]   Oxford (1970: 308).

[35]   Oxford (1970: 309).

[36]   Oxford (1970: 309-10).

[37]   Oxford (1970: 310-11).

[38]   From *On Morality* in 1885 (Fukuzawa, 1988: 79).

[39]   Kumagai (1998: 27).

[40]   Kumagai (1998: 29).

[41]   Paine (2002).

[42]   Pyle (1998: 121).

[43]   Craig (1968: 111-12).

[44]   Fukuzawa (1899: 277).

[45]   Zhang argues that the reason of the reasons for China's self-humiliations over such a long period is due to the lack of spirit of independence among the Chinese peoples. The formation of the Chinese solid servility is partially due to the Manchurian ruling during before the fall of the Qing dynasty.

[46]   This observation is proper. But behind the phenomenon, the "efforts" against Western penetration and the "policy" of giving up some parts of China to the Western powers (rather than modernizing national arm) were the rational (perhaps the best) strategies for the Manchurian group to continue ruling the (Han) Chinese. Different from Japan whose emperor was Japanese, if China was westernized at that time, the Manchurians would "automatically" lose the monopolistic power over China.

[47]   Tooyama (1998: 241). As observed by Hirota (2001), according to whether they appreciate or criticize Japan's modernization, scholars can be roughly classified into two groups. Those who positively appreciate Japan's modernization tend to positively value Fukuzawa, and vice versa.

[48]    Fukuzawa (1899: 296).[49]    Since 1978, China has been following many ways that Fukuzawa suggested so long ago.

[50]    Fukuzawa (1885).

[51]    Blacker (1968: 137).

[52]    In his 1878 letter to Nakamura Ritsuen (Fukuzawa, 1985: 112).

[53]    In *Gakumon no Susume* (Fukuzawa, 1985: 71-2).

## 7 Fukuzawa Modernized Manifestations of the Ancient Confucianism

[1]    It should be noted that there were some other important Japanese Enlightenment thinkers living in Fukuzawa's time (see, for instance, Blacker, 1969: Chap. 4, Beasley, 1995: Chaps. 4 and 5). As Macfarlane (2002) warns, "Like all great thinkers, it is false to isolate Fukuzawa. He was part of a network. Yet by general consent he is the greatest of them. …"

[2]    Blacker (1986: 68).

[3]    It can be shown that Chinese have always respected intellectuals who perceive this world based on emotion rather than rational analysis. This is a main reason that Mainland Chinese have failed to sustain a high civilization in modern times.

[4]    In my courses I often use the persons printed in the three notes, Chinese 100 Yuan, Japanese 10,000 yen, and American 100 dollars, to illustrate the behavioral mechanisms of the Mainland Chinese, the Japanese, and the Americans.

[5]    My recent book (Zhang, 2007) examines China's problems from broad perspectives.

[6]    Fukuzawa wrote an essay entitled "The pursuit of learning is merely one among hundreds of human games." See Nisikawa and Yamauchi (2002: 169-71).

[7]    Tamaki (2001: 177) quotes one criticism against Fukuzawa: "Those who believe blindly in him may call him 'the Sage of Mita'. But in fact he is not a pure scholar but in fact 'the merchant of learning' instead.…Those who earn from learning should be called 'merchant of learning'. He is indeed one of the most prominent of these merchants

of learning." He did not want to become a pure scholar and he judged himself to be "shallow" in thought. Instead of all these, he should be considered as the pioneer of East Asia's Westernization.

[8]    *Questions on Moral Education* published in 1882 (Fukuzawa, 159-61).

[9]    Pyle (1998: 104).

[10]   In his 1878 letter to Nakamura Ritsuen (Fukuzawa, 1985: 113).

[11]   Kiyooka (1985: 3).

[12]   It should be remarked that in *Japan versus China in the Industrial Race*, Zhang (1998) also emphasizes another significant difference between Japan and China when the two countries were faced with challenges from the West. China was under the control of the Manchus, while Japan was racially harmonious.

[13]   De Bary (2003: 361).

[14]   Smith (1988: 135).

[15]   Fukuzawa (1985: 158-9).

[16]   Fukuzawa (1985: 159).

[17]   Each of the principles is examined in detail in Zhang (1999).

[18]   Yao (2000: 248).

[19]   Cook and Rosemont (1994: 47).

[20]   Indeed, Karl Marx will laugh at the so-called Chinese Marxism if he had chance to read Chinese official interpretations of his thought. Similarly, ancient Confucianists perhaps would not agree with what the neo-Confucianists advocated.

[21]   In particular, I could not help feeling the echo when I was comparing Hsün Tzu (298-238 BC) and Fukuzawa. Hsün Tzu built his rational Confucian system on the assumption that human nature is evil. It should be remarked that since long time ago this great man had been almost neglected both in East Asia and the West.

[22]   Tsuzumi (2000: 466). *Sonno* culture refers to the culture of emperor worship, which survived Japan's defeat in 1945.

[23]   Wakabayashi (1998: 4-5).

[24]   Wakabayashi (1998: 5).

[25]   Kumagai (1998: 23).

[26]   Kumagai (1998: 23).

[27]    Nishimura's early education was based on the Confucian classics but included Western learning as well. He did not support the Meiji Restoration of 1868, yet he later entered the new imperial government and became a major figure in the government to educate the Japanese on the essentials of Western civilization. In 1890 he was selected as an imperial appointee to he House of Peers.

[28]    Shivelly (1965: 238).

[29]    Blacker (1968: 65).

[30]    Schopenhauer (1958 I: 230-1).

# Biblography

Blacker, C. (1968) Foreword, in The Autobiography of Yukichi Fukuzawa, translated by Kiyooka, E. New York: Columbia University Press.

Blacker, C. (1969) The Japanese Enlightenment: A Study of the Writings of Fukuzawa Yukichi. London: Cambridge University Press, 1969.

Blacker, C. (2000) Collected Writings of Carmen Blacker. Tokyo: Edition Synapse.

Chen, H.C. (1911) The Economic Principles of Confucius and His School. New York: The Faculty of Political Science of Columbia University.

Chigusa, Y. (1994). The Economic Thought of Fukuzawa Yukichi: The Contemporary Implications. Oda : Kanton Gakuen University.

Chamberlain, B.H. (1904) Japanese Things, Being Notes on Various Subjects Connected with Japan. 1990, Tokyo: Tuttle.

Cook, D.J. and Roscmont, H. (1994) Introduction Writings on China, see Leibniz (1994).

Craig, A.M. (1968) Fukuzawa Yukichi – The Philosophical Foundations of Meiji Nationalism, in Political Development in Modern Japan, edited by Ward, R.E. Princeton: Princeton University Press.

De Bary, W.T. (2003) Why Confucius Now? in Confucianism for the Modern World, edited by Bell, D.A. and Chairbong, H. Cambridge: Cambridge University Press.

Drucker, P. F. (2001) Why the Men of Meiji Are Important Today, The preface in Peter Drucker and Fukuzawa Yukichi, by Mochituki, M. Tokyo: Shodensha.

Englander, F. (2002) Fukuzawa Yukichi – His Attack upon Confucian Doctrine of Meibun and Within Japanese Families. http://mll.kenyon.edu/~japanese02/J28sp99/ projects/ englander/1/ .

Fujitani, T. (1989) The Kokka Shinto and the Tenno. Kyoto: The Research Institute of Community.

Fukuzawa Y. (1875) An Outline of a Theory of Civilization, translated by David A. Dilworth, D. A. and Hurst, G.C., reprinted in The Japanese Discovery of America: A Brief History With Documents, edited by Duus, P, 1997. Boston: Bedford.

Fukuzawa, Y. (1885) Good-bye Asia, in Japan: A Documentary History, edited by David Lu, D. 1997. Armonk: M. E. Sharpe.

Fukuzawa, Y. (1899) The Autobiography of Yukichi Fukuzawa, translated by Kiyooka, E., 1968. New York: Columbia University Press.

Fukuzawa, Y. (1985) Fukuzawa Yukichi on Education – Selected Works, translated and edited by Kiyooka, E. Tokyo: University of Tokyo Press.

Fukuzawa, Y. (1988) Fukuzawa Yukichi on Japanese Women – Selected Works, translated and edited by Kiyooka, E. Tokyo: University of Tokyo Press.

Fuziwara, A. (1993) The Political Economics of Francis Wayland: The Modern Japan, Fukuzawa and Wayland. Tokyo: Nihon Keizai Hyouronsha Ltd.

Fuziwara, A. (1998) Fukuzawa Yukichi on Japanese Economics. Tokyo: Nihon Keizai Hyouronsha Ltd.

Gordon, A. (1992) Labor and Imperial Democracy in Prewar Japan. Berkley: University of California.

Haltutori, R. (2003, edited) The Collections of Fukuzawa Yukichi's Writings, Vol 11. Tokyo: Keio University Press.

Hegel, G.W.F. (1991) The Philosophy of History, translated from the German original by J. Sibree. Buffalo: Prometheus Books.

Hill, C. (1972) The World Turned Upside Down: Radical Ideas During the English Revolution. New York: Viking Press.

Hirakawa, S. (1998) Japan's Turn to the West, translated by Wakabayashi, in Modern Japanese Thought, edited by Wakabayashi, B.T. London: Cambridge University Press.

Hirayama Y. (2002) Fukuzawa Yukichi's Understanding of the West and His "Datsu-A Ron", in The Diffusion of Western Thought in Japan, edited by Koizumi, T. Tokyo: Keio University Press.

Hiroshi, M. (1999) Introduction, in Western Economics in Japan: The Early Years, edited by Chuhei, S. Bristol: Thoemmes Press.

Hirota, M. (2001) On Modern Japan: Fukuzawa Yukichi and Common People and Discrimination. Tokyo: Yoshikawakoubunkan.

Hopper, H.M. (2005) Fukuzawa Yûkichi: From Samurai to Capitalist. New York: Pearson Education.

Howell, D.L. (2000) Embracing Modernity in Meiji Japan, paper presented at Teaching World History and Geography 2000, a conference at Austin, Texas, February 11-12.

Howland, D. R. (2002) Translating the West: Language and Political Reason in Noneteenth-Century Japan. Honolulu: University of Hawai'i Press.

Hsün Tzu (1994) Xunxi, A translation and study of the Complete works, by Knoblock, J. California: Stanford University Press.

Huntington, S. (1996) The Clash of Civilizations and the Remaking of World Order. New York: Touchstone.

Hume, D. (1994) Political Essays, edited by Knud Haakonssen. Cambridge: Cambridge University Press.

I Ching or Book of Changes (1993) translated by James Legge in 1899 and revised and annotate ed by Qin Ying. Hunan: Hunan Publishing House.

Iwatani, Z. and Nisikawa, S. (2003, edited) The Collections of Fukuzawa Yukichi's Writings, Vol. 8. Tokyo: Keio University Press.

Kitaoka, S. (2002) Independence and Self-respect: Challenges from Fukuzawa Yukichi. Tokyo: Kodansha.

Kiyooka, E. (1985, edited) Fukuzawa Yukichi on Education: Selected Works. Tokyo: University of Tokyo Press.

Kiyooka, E. (1988, edited) Fukuzawa Yukichi on Japanese Women: Selected Works. Tokyo: University of Tokyo Press.

Koizumi, T. (2002) Fukuzawa Yukichi on Religions. Tokyo: Keio University Press.

Komuro, M. (2003, edited) The Collections of Fukuzawa Yukichi's Writings, Vol. 6. Tokyo: Keio University Press.

Komuro, M. and Nisikawa, S. (2002, edited) The Collections of Fukuzawa Yukichi's Writings, Vol. 3. Tokyo: Keio University Press.

Kumagai, J. (1998) Enlightenment and Economic Thought in Meiji Japan: Yukichi Fukuzawa and Ukichi Taguchi, in Economic Thought and Modernization in Japan, edited by Sugihara, S. and Ranaka, T. Cheltenham: Edward Elgar.

Leibniz, G.W. (1994) Writings on China, translated by D.J. Cook and H. Rosemont. Chicago: Open Court.

Lu, D. (1997) Japan: A Documentary History, Vol. II, The Late Tokukawa Period to the Present. Armonk: M.E.Sharpe.

Lu, X. (1980) Selected Works, in four volumes, translated from the Chinese origin by X.Y. Yang and G. Yang. Beijing: Foreign Languages Press.

Macfarlane, A. (2002) The Making of the Modern World: Visions from the West and East. New York: Palgrave.

McClosky, H. and Zaller, J. (1984) The American Ethos: Public Attitudes towards Capitalism and Democracy. Mass., Cambridge: Harvard University Press.

Mencius (1992) The Works of Mencius, in The Four Book translated by James Legge and revised and annotate ed by Liu and Zhiye Luo, Hunan: Hunan Publishing House.

Miyakawa, T. (2000) The Role of Policy Analysis for Democratic Policy-Making. NIRA Review, Winter.

Montesquieu (1748) The Spirit of Laws. Edited by D.W. Carrithers, 1977, Berkeley: University of California Press.

Mungello, D.E. (1977) Leibniz and Confucianism—The Search for Accord. Honolulu: The University Press of Hawaii.

Nakayama, K. (1985) Introduction, in Fukuzawa Yukichi on Education, translated and edited by Kiyooka, E. Tokyo: University of Tokyo Press.

Nagata, M. (2003) Fukuzawa Yukichi on Science. Tokyo: Keio University Press.

Nishikawa, S. (1993) Fukuzawa Yukichi, Prospects: The Quarterly Review of Comparative Education 23, 493-506.

Nishikawa, S. (2001) Why Fukuzawa Fits the Bill. http://www.lookjapan.com/Lbecobiz /O1AprEF.htm.

Nishikawa, S. and Yamauchi, K. (2002, edited) The Collections of Fukuzawa Yukichi's Writings, Vol.5. Tokyo: Keio University Press.

Nisizawa, N. (2003, edited) The Collections of Fukuzawa Yukichi's Writings, Vol.10. Tokyo: Keio University Press.

Oxford, W.H. (1970) A Critical Edition of Selected Speeches of Fukuzawa Yukichi Dealing With the Modernization of Japan, reprinted 2001. Michigan: A Bell & Howell Company.

Paine, S. (2002) The Sino-Japanese War of 1894-1895. Annual Newsletter of the Slavic Research Centre, No. 10, December 2002. Hokkaido: Hokkaido University.

Patten, C. (1999). East and West – The Last Governor of Hong Kong on Power, Freedom and the Future. London: Pan Books.

Piovesana, S.J.G.K. (1997) Recent Japanese Philosophical Thought 1862-1996, A Survey. Surrey: Japan Library.

Pyle, K.B. (1998) Meiji Conservatism, in Modern Japanese Thought, edited by Wakabayashi, B.T. London: Cambridge University Press.

Sagers, J.H. (2006) Origins of Japanese Wealth and Power: Reconciling Confucianism and Capitalism, 1830-1885. New York: Palgrave.

Sakamoto, T. (2002, edited) The Collections of Fukuzawa Yukichi's Writings, Vol.9. Tokyo: Keio University Press.

Saucier, M. and Nisikawa, S. (2002, edited) The Collections of Fukuzawa Yukichi's Writings, Vol.1. Tokyo: Keio University Press.

Schopenhauer, A. (1958) The World as Will and Representation, in two volumes, translated from the German by E.F.J. Payne. New York: Dover Publications.

Shen, Z.H. (1998) China Sends Troops to Korea: Beijing's Policy-Making Process, in China and the United States – A New Cold War History, edited by Li, X.B. and Li, H.S. New York: University Press of America.

Shively, D.H. (1965) Nishimura Shigeki: A Confucian View of Modernization, in Changing Japanese Attitudes Toward Modernization, edited by Jansen, M.B. Princeton: Princeton University Press.

Smith, A. (1759) The Theory of Moral Sentiments, edited by D.D. Raphael and A.L. Macfie, 1982. Indianapolis: Liberty Press.

Smith, T.C. (1988) Native Sources of Japanese Industrialization. Berkley: University of California Press.

Sugiyama, C. (1986) The Political Economic Thought During the Meiji Enlightenment Period: With Fukuzawa Yukichi as the Central Figure. Tokyo: Hosei University Press.

Tamaki, N. (2001) Yukichi Fukuzawa, 1835-1901: The Sprit of Enterprise in Modern Japan. New York: Palgrave.

Tamaki, N. (2002) Yukichi Fukuzawa, 1835-1901: Learn and Earn, Earn and Learn. Tokyo: Yuhikaku.

Terasaki, O. (2003, edited) The Collections of Fukuzawa Yukichi's Writings, Vol.7. Tokyo: Keio University Press.

The Classic of Filial Piety. Shangdon: Shangdon Friendship Press.

The Great Learning (1992) in The Four Book translated by James Legge and revised and annotated by Zhongde Liu and Zhiye Luo, Hunan: Hunan Publishing House.

Tocqueville, A.de. (1835) Democracy in America, translated from the French origin by Lawrence, G, 1990. Chicago: Encyclopedia Britannica, INC.

Tooyama, S. (1998) Fukuzawa Yukichi: The Relations between Thought and Politics. Tokyo: Tokyo University Press.

Tozawa, Y. (2002, edited) The Collections of Fukuzawa Yukichi's Writings, Vol. 4. Tokyo: Keio University Press.

Tsuzuki, C. (2000) The Pursuit of Power in Modern Japan, 1825-1995. Oxford: Oxford University Press.

Wakabayashi, B.T. (1998) Introduction, in Modern Japanese Thought, edited by Wakabayashi, B.T. London: Cambridge University Press.

Weber, M. (1951) The Religion of China—Confucianism and Taoism, translated from the German original by H.H. Gerth with an introduction by C.K. Yang. New York: The Free Press.

Yagi, K. (2003) Japanese Theory of Modern/Industrialization Between Liberalism and Developmentalism. http://www.siue.edu/EASTASIA/Yagi_110800.htm.

Yao, X. (1996) Confucianism and Christianity. Brighton: Academic Press.

Yasukawa, Z. (2002) Fukuzawa Yukichi's Ideas on Asia: Reconstructing Modern Japan's History. Tokyo: Koubunken.

Yonehara, K. (2003) Nationality and Christianity in Modern Japan: 'Self' and 'Others' in Japanese Political Thought, OSIPP Discussion Paper: DP-2003-E-006. Osaka: Osaka School of International Public Polity.

Zhang, W.B. (1998) Japan versus China in the Industrial Race. London: Macmillan.

Zhang, W.B. (1999) Confucianism and Industrialization. London: Macmillan.

Zhang, W.B (2000) Adam Smith and Confucius—*The Theory of Moral Sentiments* and *The Analects*. New York: Nova Science.

Zhang, W.B. (2002) Singapore's Modernization – Westernization and Modernizing Confucian Manifestations. New York: Nova Science.

Zhang, W.B. (2003a) The American Civilization Portrayed by Ancient Confucianism. New York: Algora Publisher.

Zhang, W.B. (2003b) Taiwan's Modernization. Singapore: World Scientific.

Zhang, W.B. (2006) Hong Kong – The Pearl Made of the British Mastery and the Chinese Docile-Diligence. New York: Nova Science.

Zhang, W.B. (2007) New China's Long March from Servility to Freedom. New York: Nova Science. New York: Nova Science.

CPSIA information can be obtained at www.ICGtesting.com
Printed in the USA
LVOW06s2314170114

369900LV00001B/158/P